PRAISE FOR ST
NOTHING

"*Start Chasing* Nothing is pure magic. I honestly couldn't put it down. Elaine brilliantly conveys profoundly life-changing knowledge and easily implementable tools within the context of her own fascinating life story and journey of self-discovery. It has transformed my life."

Debra Poneman
Author of *Chicken Soup for the American Idol Soul*
Founder/CEO, Yes to Success, Inc.
www.YesToSuccess.com

"*Start Chasing Nothing*" is a delightful and easy read, full of anecdotes, lessons, and insights.

Elaine Chung points the way to finding life's joy and peace from within for anyone plagued by daily dread and sadness for no reason. She reminds us that happiness is not to be found in the outer circumstances, and I applaud Elaine's courage in sharing powerful stories about how she's found happiness and peace through challenging situations in her life.

This book will show you that your ordinary aha moments can light the way to your deep inner knowing and peace."

Marci Shimoff
International Speaker

"If everything in your life appears to be good on the outside, yet you're miserable and lost on the inside, then *Start Chasing Nothing* is for you.

Elaine puts into words what so many women feel but don't dare to express—How do I get off the hamster wheel of chasing happiness?

Join Elaine on the journey so many people share to shift from suffering to peace one second at a time."

"In her book *Start Chasing Nothing*, Elaine Chung has captured many beautiful ways to find great happiness, peace of mind, and joy through the happenings of everyday life.

Her crisp, straightforward, and accessible approach to transforming our perspective in life is delightful and engaging. It's sure to win you over.

Begin to embody your greatness with this heartfelt guide. Live the life you've always imagined possible. Thank you, Elaine!"

"In her book, *Start Chasing Nothing*, Elaine Chung shares how anyone can attain happiness and inner peace right now.

By simply turning our attention within, instead of chasing something that we think will give us fulfillment in the future, we can be happy now.

Elaine candidly and with characteristically good humor, shares her transformational journey from a life of constant emotional distress to one of happiness. She offers practical tools to help us find our way back to the place of true happiness and inner peace that is always here within us.

As someone who has witnessed Elaine's profound transformation over the years I have known her, I highly recommend this book to everyone as an enjoyable and profound resource for finding peace and fulfillment."

"From the moment that I first met Elaine Chung in 2019 at the Art of Living Ashram in India, I was captured by her joy and vibrancy. The chronicle of her journey from desperation to delighting in life is an excellent roadmap for those looking for a direct route to self-discovery, personal empowerment, and fulfillment—both worldly and spiritual.

Start Chasing Nothing reads like an absorbing novel punctuated by lessons that allow personal growth to truly be a lifelong learning extravaganza. I recommend this book most highly!"

Ronnie Newman, Ed.M., C.A.S.
Director, Research and Health Promotion, Art of Living Foundation
Faculty, Nova Southeastern University,
Lifelong Learning Institute, Florida
Honorary Faculty, Sri Sri University, Orissa, India

"Elaine's story is a testament to the core principle of neuro-linguistic programming (NLP), which is, we all have the resources we need to make positive changes in our life.

In times of need, we help ourselves by first reaching for our resources from within—this is what you'll find in *Start Chasing Nothing*. Within the pages of Elaine's book, you'll discover The Formula that's the key for those wanting to access their own inner strength.

Start Chasing Nothing is easy to read and soothing. Her aha moments are inspiring, and her stories entirely relatable."

Talis Wong
Certified Global NLP Trainer
Founder & Director, DD Centre — Centre for
creating positive influence

"This book empowers people to look within themselves to find peace and happiness.
It is an easy-to-read book full of practical tips to help people shift from pain to peace. The Emergency List that Elaine introduces is a simple yet powerful tool. I strongly recommend *Start Chasing Nothing* to anyone who is looking for a way to attain lasting inner peace and fulfillment."

Sook Hyung Paek
Professional Certified Coach (PCC)
Leadership coach for transformation and change
Co-managing partner, Baobab Executive Coaching
www.BaobabExecutiveCoaching.com

"From the very first words, *Start Chasing Nothing* invites you in.

Elaine Chung draws you into her world like a best friend by painting beautifully descriptive pictures with her words.

In her book, Elaine is profoundly honest. She openly talks about her life experiences on her way to finding happiness. As you read, there is no doubt Elaine deeply understands the longing and struggle present for all those seeking inner peace and lasting happiness.

Along with her story, Elaine offers beautifully simple guidance and practical techniques to help you on your own journey."

Kathryn Johnson
Bestselling author of *The Joy of Obstacles*
www.inspiredbykathryn.com

Start Chasing Nothing

Start Chasing Nothing is a book written for people who want lasting happiness through the happenings of everyday life.

It is a practical guide filled with life-changing knowledge and easy to use techniques to help anyone plagued by daily dread to find joy and peace from within.

The three-step Formula and the Emergency List introduced in this book are transformative and help you calm what disturbs you and return you to your inner source of wisdom and strength.

You'll learn how to use the Formula to go inward to discover the source from which all happiness flows. The Emergency List helps you shift from turmoil to peace, one second at a time. These techniques help us simply turn our attention within, and be happy now, instead of chasing something that we think will give us fulfillment in the future.

It doesn't matter if your life is ordinary or extraordinary. It doesn't matter if you have a little money or a lot. The only thing you need is a desire to attain lasting inner peace and fulfilment. The Formula and Emergency List will help you be happy from the inside out, so you can stop relying on outside factors which will only keep you chasing but won't give you lasting happiness and fulfillment.

Start Chasing Nothing

*A Guide to Lasting Happiness
and Inner Peace*

ELAINE CHUNG

WITH DR. SUSAN L. REID

Published by
Hybrid Global Publishing
301 E 57th Street
4th Floor
New York, NY 10022

Manufactured in the United States of America.

Chung, Elaine
Start Chasing Nothing: A Guide to Lasting Happiness and Inner Peace
    ISBN: 978-1-951943-83-7
    eBook: 978-1-951943-84-4
    LCCN: 2021921278

Cover design by: Natasha Clawson
Copyediting by: XCU Agency
Proofreading by: Dea Gunning
Interior design by: Suba Murugan

Disclaimer:

Elaine@startchasingnothing.com

—This book is dedicated to—

those who need reminding that true happiness is found within you

ACKNOWLEDGMENTS

Writing a book is more complex than I thought, and more rewarding than I could have ever imagined.

None of this would have been possible without the love and support of my husband, who's always been my rock and my muse. And my two boys, who are my teachers and my joy in life. Thank you for all the love we share, the fun we have together, and always the laughter. Above all, thanks for convincing me that eight legs are better than two!

I'm eternally grateful for my sister. Your kindness and care throughout, not only during this writing process but in life, have meant more to me than words can say. Many hugs and much love.

Thank you, Mom and Dad, for your patience and for giving me space to be who I am. Thanks also to my brother for the biggest life lesson of forgiveness, which I'm still learning.

To my Ah Mah, although you are no longer with us, your gifts and lessons still live on within me. Although I never got a chance to thank you, I will be forever grateful.

Much love to my cousin, Charis Chung, for believing I was a good person during the bleak times when I did not believe so myself. Your faith in me, prayers for me, and continued support buoy me. Always. Thanks for holding open the space and shining the light.

Writing a book is much like birthing a baby.

I owe an enormous debt of gratitude to those who've walked with me as I birthed myself. Debra Poneman, I couldn't have asked for a more incredible or loving mentor. You've shown me the light, been my role model, and are the one I want to be like when I finally grow up.

Everyone needs someone in their life who encourages them to be themselves. My coach, Suzanne Lawlor, is that person for me. Thank you for illuminating my blind spots, and for teaching me how to be kind to myself.

Thank you, Marci Shimoff, for showing me the way to be happy. For no reason! You are a tremendous inspiration. Thank you, Dr. Sue Morter for pointing me to live in the front side of the model. And to Lisa Garr, for reminding me to become more aware instead of just going through the motions in life.

Many thanks to my NLP teacher and friend, Talis Wong. I have learned so much from you over the years. Not just about NLP, but about life and right living. Thanks for generously sharing your knowledge and showing by example.

It really does take a village to write a book.

Without my very good friend, Sook Hyung Paek, encouraging me every step of the way, there'd be no book to read. You saw the goodness in me when I couldn't. You're like a bottle of vitamins in human form. I always feel nourished after a conversation with you. Everyone needs a Sook in their life!

Many thanks to Dr. Susan L. Reid, who brilliantly transformed my thoughts into words. Thanks for pushing me to the finish line!

Sayuri Ichikawa, thank you for being such a terrific sounding board at the beginning phase of this project. Thanks for allowing me to bounce ideas off you and believing in me and the book I just *had* to write.

Special thanks to my good friends, Winnie Suen, Diana Tu, April Tang, Sue Shelley, Kathryn Johnson, Paula Qi and Aditi Ahalpara. Your kindness and support gave me strength not only in writing this book but in walking this life with my head up.

I have made so many good friends and met many beautiful people through The Art of Living Foundation. Special thanks to my Gurudev Sri Sri Ravi Shankar for your blessings. Thank you for showing me the beauty in silence and that unconditional love and kindness are possible.

I also thank all the teachers and healers who helped me on my path, including John Newton, Master John Douglas, Amshiva, Ronnie Newman, and everyone at The Sedona Method.

I'm immensely grateful to my sisters from my Year of Miracles group: Wendy Nichols, Muriel Soden, and Janice Ong. Thanks for your wise counsel and intentions.

I cannot express enough thanks to everyone at HKICPA. You're like a second family to me.

Finally, I offer up special thanks and appreciation for the spiritual beings in my heart to whom I give thanks every day: Jesus Christ, Bhagavan Krishna, Mahavatar Babaji, Lahiri Mahasaya, Swami Sri Yukteswar, and Paramahansa Yogananda. Thank you for all the gifts I've received and the lessons that have helped me grow. Thank you, for I know you answer when I call.

CONTENTS

FOREWORD

I first met Elaine Chung in 2017 when she made the trek from Hong Kong to San Francisco, California, to attend a four-day Yes to Success program I held in my home called, Living Your Truth, Becoming the Light.

I was impressed that Elaine was so committed to her transformation that she was willing to fly 7,000 miles to the other side of the world to be a part of an event that, by the time she had recovered from jet lag, would be practically over.

As one day turned into the next, I got to know Elaine better and fell in love with her quiet beauty and intelligence. She told us about the chronic self-doubt that haunted her, and how she woke up each morning filled with dread about the day to come. She also shared the life-changing health scare that allowed her to realize that she had to find fulfillment within.

As the program progressed, ever self-effacing, Elaine reluctantly revealed her credentials as a highly accomplished, multi-degreed professional with a résumé a mile long. By the time our four days ended, it was crystal clear what drove this talented, insightful woman—she wanted to be happy and was on a do-or-die mission to discover how. In the pages of *Start Chasing Nothing*, you'll find that this mission has been gloriously accomplished. In this brilliant book, you'll not only learn the source of Elaine's self-doubt, but why it is a universal malady in our world today—especially for women.

You'll also discover that The Formula Elaine developed can turn your life around as it did for her. In fact, The Formula worked so well for Elaine that I now count her as one of the happiest people I know. When we met up in India in 2019, just before COVID-19 stopped the world, our days together were filled with non-stop laughter and adventure. Her joy is positively disarming!

If that is the kind of transformation you want in your life, you have my word that you'll find the key in *Start Chasing Nothing*.

This isn't a dry "how-to" book. It's an exciting wellspring of inspiration and tools for personal growth. Elaine skillfully weaves her techniques for transformation into her life's story, and that story happens to be so fascinating that you won't be able to put the book down.

It almost feels like a bonus that you're given every tool you need to shift your consciousness from one filled with frustration, self-doubt, and perhaps even despair, to become one filled with deep knowing that all is well and all possibilities await you!

While reading Elaine's book, one of the things that struck me deeply was how courageous she was to share the story of her pain and struggle. Her degree of vulnerability took my breath away. I found it incredibly inspiring how she goes to such a beautiful, raw space and opens up about all the feelings that most of us keep hidden—and this from a woman who comes from a background where "one does not speak of these things."

I know you'll be able to relate to Elaine's struggles, disappointments, and the emptiness she's felt, and more than once you'll say to yourself, "If she can create a great life, I can too!"

There is no one more qualified than Elaine to write this book. She has resolutely applied The Formula to every aspect of her life, and uses her Emergency List daily. Countless others have also used The Formula and substantiated that what Elaine teaches really works.

There's no need to live with self-doubt or fear, and there's no need to suffer.

Let Elaine show you how to See, Stop, Be Still, and Shift. It's that simple. I invite you to take the plunge into *Start Chasing Nothing*. I'm confident it holds the answers you seek.

Debra Poneman

Founder, Yes to Success, Inc.

PREFACE

I remember it clearly. It was a gorgeous, white-powdered morning. I was just waking up and could hear my husband in the kitchen making breakfast. My two boys were putting on their ski pants and talking in excitedly hushed voices about which black diamond runs they were going to do today.

I should have been happy.

It was winter break for the boys, and we were in Niseko, Japan, taking our annual ski holiday at Mount Yotei. My boys, then seventeen and thirteen, are avid skiers and snowboarders. Although it is a long trek from our home in Hong Kong—a seven-hour flight plus a three-hour coach ride—it's something our whole family looks forward to all year long.

This particular year, we were staying at the Landmark View Apartments, which have ceiling-to-floor windows that offer a spectacular view of Mt. Yotei from the balcony. With only a three-minute walk to the Hirafu Gondola, we were in the perfect location.

Or, my body was.

My mind was in a completely different spot.

Morning Dread

What I hadn't told anyone, even my husband, was that for years I'd been waking up feeling dread.

You know how some people have Sunday night dread—that pit-in-your-stomach feeling as you contemplate going back to work the next

XXIV • *Start Chasing Nothing*

day? Well, I had that every morning. No, I'm not exaggerating. *Every* morning. It's called Morning Dread.

Neuroscientist Lisa Feldman Barrett talks about this in her book, *How Emotions Are Made.* She describes Morning Dread as "being held hostage to spiraling a.m. anxiety."[1] It's caused by "your brain reacting to physical sensations you're feeling in the form of emotions."[2] And it's debilitating.

So, here I was on a wonderful ski holiday with my family feeling dread, and begging God to help me get up.

What was wrong with me?

I Can't Breathe

On so many occasions when I was at home, at work, out with friends, exercising, or even taking a walk, I'd find myself unable to breathe.

It didn't matter if I was typing on the computer keyboard at work or meditating at home, out of nowhere, and at the most innocuous times, I'd feel my throat constrict. Soon I'd be gasping for air as my hands pulled at a too-tight collar I wasn't wearing.

What was happening to me?

I had a job that I loved, a family I adored, enough money to live comfortably, and good health. I'd done everything I was supposed to do—made good grades, majored in business, became a certified public accountant, and finally earned a law degree at university, married a wonderful man, had two sons, progressed up the corporate ladder, and took good care of myself and my family. So why was I waking up every morning with bone-numbing dread and thoughts of ending my life?

Now, of course, I really wouldn't end my life. Still, as ashamed of myself as I am to say it...the thought was there. Constantly.

Hamster Wheel Life

I know it sounds cliché; nonetheless, I was the hamster in the wheel.

I seriously believed that if I did more, I'd have more, and then I'd be happy. I knew there was something wrong with this thinking, yet I was too busy to do anything about it.

Habit 7 in Stephen Covey's *The 7 Habits of Highly Effective People* is taking time to sharpen the saw:

> Suppose you were to come upon someone in the woods working feverishly to saw down a tree.
>
> "What are you doing?" you ask.
>
> "Can't you see?" comes the impatient reply. "I'm sawing down this tree."
>
> "You look exhausted!" you exclaim. "How long have you been at it?"
>
> "Over five hours," he returns, "and I'm beat! This is hard work."
>
> "Well, why don't you take a break for a few minutes and sharpen that saw?" you inquire. "I'm sure it would go a lot faster."
>
> "I don't have time to sharpen the saw," the man says emphatically. "I'm too busy sawing!"[3]

This was me!

It seemed that no matter how hard I worked or how much I achieved, it still wasn't enough.

I begged God to help me get up in the morning, and I went through my hamster wheel day on fumes, only to wake up and do it all again. I was a Busy. Aimless. Hamster.

Contrast that with how grateful and blessed I felt for my wonderful family and career. I knew I had an enviable life. Yet, day after day, year after year, I awoke with that sick feeling in the pit of my stomach of dread and foreboding. It was all I could do to not throw myself out the window.

Life was pointless.

Wasn't I supposed to be happy?

Chasing Happiness

You know that country song from the '80s, *Lookin' for Love*, by Johnny Lee? It was about looking for love in all the wrong places.

That was me.

Except that I was looking for happiness in all the wrong places. And I felt miserable.

I was good at chasing approval and validation. I was good at buying things and taking holidays. I was very good at focusing outside myself on things and people external to myself, to make me happy. As the song says—*in all the wrong places*.

And I also blamed people and things for making me unhappy. I'm not proud of this.

When things went wrong, I made excuses, looked for faults in people, work, and even myself. And then I'd jump back on the wheel and chase things that would make me happy. Buy more things. Take more holidays. More. More. More.

Psychologists call this external locus of control.

People who attribute their success and happiness to outside influences have an external locus of control. Whereas people with an internal locus of control take responsibility for their actions.

I desperately needed to get off the hamster wheel and sharpen my axe.

My "Aha" Moment

People talk about having earth-shattering aha moments All. The. Time.

Not me.

My aha moment was way less grand.

According to Merriam-Webster, an aha moment is defined as "A moment of sudden inspiration, insight, recognition, or comprehension."[4]

Some people have "lightbulb" moments with little hairs on their arms standing up. Others, a feeling of "euphoric eureka" when a sudden understanding pops into their mind.

Nope. Not me.

My aha moment was more of an inner knowing, similar to how Oprah Winfrey talks about what the aha moment means to her:

> The thing about an aha moment is that you think you've never thought of it that way before...But you can't have an 'aha' unless you already knew it. So, aha is the remembering of what you already knew, articulated in a way to resonate with your own truth. So, the aha isn't somebody teaching you something; the aha is...remembering.[5]

So, there I was, waking up on a gorgeous, white-powdered morning with my husband in the kitchen and the boys pulling on ski pants. That familiar, sick feeling of dread inside.

Then it happened.

For just a moment, like a train changing tracks, I was off the wheel.

Nothing earth-shattering or spiritually spectacular. Just a little bump as my train shifted to another track.

What Happened Next

The moment I was off the wheel, I knew, deep inside, that how I felt had nothing to do with the external world. After all, I was on a perfect holiday with the people I love most. Nothing was wrong, yet I still felt sad. Therefore, the problem must come from within me.

The dread I felt each morning, throat constrictions throughout the day, and exhaustion at night wasn't going to go away by me chasing external approval and validation, or my buying more things and going on another holiday.

It would stop when I quit chasing,

And start when I journeyed inward.

Inward to find my truth.

Inward to discover happiness.

Inward to bring a level of spiritual awareness to all that I do, be, and have.

I'm not going to tell you that after my aha moment everything painful went "poof," or that my train never shifted back to its hamster wheel track. What I am going to tell you is that we're in this together, dear reader.

It's an inside job for both of us.

After all, your journey and mine are one and the same.

INTRODUCTION

*Be aware of your inner voice and follow it, even though most of
the time it will tell you the most uncomfortable path to choose.*

Glenn Close

This book would not let me go.

I had to write.

Has something like this ever happened to you? Where you know, deep down inside, that you have to do something. Like a calling. Until it's downright unpleasant! And the more you don't do it, the louder and more urgent that calling becomes.

Well, that's what happened to me.

What started as a slight niggling that I ignored and passed off as a whim turned into a raging, relentless nagging in my mind, and a burning desire in my heart. It would not Let. Me. Go! I was possessed from within with uncertainty and battered from without by doubts and insecurities.

I was a mess.

I made excuses for why I wasn't writing, placed other mundane things before writing—like laundry and running errands—and told myself I'd start writing tomorrow.

Days turned into weeks. Weeks turned into months. Then years!

This waffling back and forth between conviction and procrastination was exhausting. I had writer's block *before* I started writing. Is that even possible?

While I procrastinated and made excuses for not writing, my inner voice kept nudging. Incessantly. Like a dog that won't let go of a bone, *Start Chasing Nothing* wouldn't let go of me.

Ignore the Croaking Chorus

Dale Carnegie, a pioneer of the self-improvement genre, says it best: "If you have some idea you believe in, don't listen to the croaking chorus. Listen to what your own inner voice tells you."

Okay. Let's do this!

I listened to my inner voice and made writing this book a high priority. I started waking up at 5:00 A.M. every day to write, even though it meant that I only wrote an hour before heading out for the ferry on workdays. On weekends, I wrote for lengthier periods. I was in the zone, and it felt amazingly good and right.

In his memoir, *On Writing*, Stephen King explains, "I did it for the pure joy of the thing. And if you can do it for joy, you can do it forever."[1]

In short, it took me two years to pluck up the courage to ignore the "croaking of the chorus" and listen to my inner voice. And nine full months to complete as I juggled family and work with the demands of writing. Yet, it's all been worth it!

As you read this book, you'll laugh, cry, smile, nod, and resonate with my journey and the experiences of my family and friends (whose... names and other identifying markers are changed to honor their privacy). Your heart will go out to us all as you recognize yourself within the pages of our experiences.

We are all in this together, dear reader.

I'm a Prius

There are three things essential for you to know at the start of our journey. The first is that I consider myself a Prius.

A hybrid.

What this means is that I'm a product of both Eastern and Western cultures. I was born in Hong Kong to Chinese parents. I lived there until I was ten, when my parents, older brother and sister, and I emigrated to Canada.

I was the only Chinese in my class and spoke no English. To survive, I quickly learned how to speak English, and function in a culture very different from the one I knew.

I wasn't allowed to speak English at home because my parents were worried that I would forget my mother tongue.

I went to university in British Columbia, and have worked in Vancouver and Singapore. In 1997, after living in Canada for fifteen years, I moved back to Hong Kong for work. Here, I met my Scottish husband, and together we're raising two wonderful boys.

Onward from age ten, I've had to work in, live in, and balance two cultures simultaneously.

I speak Cantonese and English. I write Chinese and English. My family and I are an amalgamation of Eastern and Western cultures.

Sounds pretty cool, right?

Well, here's the thing—for a long time, I didn't feel as if I belonged in either world.

I was bullied as a kid in school because I didn't fit in. At home, I was teased for being a tomboy and resisting conventional rules. I came from a family with traditional Chinese values, and I had to work hard to fit in at home.

As I grew older, it just got worse. In my family, tremendous value was placed on listening to and respecting your elders. I wanted to please my parents by being obedient, studious, and a straight-A student. I wanted to fit in—not stand out. Growing up, bouncing back and forth between two cultures while trying to fit in made me feel unsure about myself.

You can see how my insecurity about standing out haunted me as I wrote this book. *Who was I to write a book? What could I possibly have to*

XXXII • *Start Chasing Nothing*

say? After all, books come from people who've had extraordinary experiences. Not from lil' ol' me.

Today, I think of myself as a Prius: a fully hybrid, traditional Chinese woman with Western ideas. I embody the best of both worlds. I honor my cultural heritage, and I celebrate the freedom to be me.

As you read this book, I encourage you to be a Prius, too. Embrace your past and meld it with your present. Take whatever makes you unique and sets you apart, and know that you deserve to be happy.

Mind Stories

The second essential thing is that throughout *Start Chasing Nothing*, I talk about the crazy stories our minds make up when we're hurt, angry, or in distress. Often called "monkey mind," it's a term that refers to the mind when it's unsettled, restless, or confused. Also called the "inner critic," the monkey mind keeps you from living in the present. It's the part of your brain most connected to the ego, which contends that you can't do anything right and will never be good enough. It keeps you stuck in a negative mind story, looping around and around, and preventing you from moving forward.

Even though the mind is a wonderful thing, it can get in the way of what your heart wants to say. The whole point of *Start Chasing Nothing* is to train yourself to see the negative chatter in your mind for what it is—your mind is either freaking out about the future or stuck in the past—and grounding yourself in your body so you can listen to your heart.

Since the mind dwells in the past and future, and the body resides in the present, you'll learn how to center yourself within your body in *Start Chasing Nothing*.

Stop Chasing—Start Flowing

The third essential thing is that this book talks a lot about chasing and the pain it causes. Right up front, I want you to know that chasing is not the same as seeking.

Seeking implies questing. A seeking of inner truth. The discovery of your inner voice, which in turn, leads to happiness. It's a wholesome, open-hearted way of moving with the current rather than against it.

Chasing has a much different energy. It's singularly focused with a blinkered perspective. Sure, it can bring you external recognition and trophies to hang on your wall, and can even make you feel as if you're happy—for a while. Yet, it is fleeting. Chasing always requires more, and the genesis of true happiness isn't found by chasing more.

I like how Abraham-Hicks talks about the stream of well-being that flows from non-physical source:

> "Imagine taking your canoe down to the river's edge. A very nice, fast-moving stream. Your paddles are already attached to your boat as you put it in the water. Then, you deliberately turn it upstream and begin paddling very hard against this fast-moving current.
> And we say, "why not just turn and go with the flow?"
> Doesn't that seem lazy? My mother wouldn't approve of that. Or my teachers. They've all had me pointing the other way. In fact, every plaque on my wall was based on paddling upstream. And I was measured against the others who did it, too. And the better we did it, the bigger the trophies.
> Nothing that you want is upstream. And when you buck the current, it beats up on you pretty good.

The stream of well-being is a powerful stream, and it takes you downstream. And when you let yourself go with it, you have a glorious ride. But when you paddle against it, you feel unfulfilled, dissatisfied, overwhelmed, fearful, and discouraged."

Chasing causes pain.

Going with the flow results in happiness.

The Formula

Central to *Start Chasing Nothing* is The Formula.

The Formula is a simple three-step process that quickly helps you stop yourself from focusing on the mind stories, and to restore inner peace and calm. These three steps will profoundly impact your life:

Step One—See
Step Two—Stop and Be Still
Step Three—Shift

Throughout *Start Chasing Nothing*, I talk about how The Formula will help you return to center and how it will focus your attention inward for balance. I use two examples to illustrate these points. The first is the Weeble.

Remember the Weeble? That roly-poly toy that Hasbro introduced in the '70s. Shaped like an egg with a weighted bottom, it always bounced back to its upright position when hit.

That's what The Formula will do for you. It guides you through the steps that will help you get back up, no matter what hits you've taken, so that like the Weeble, while you may wobble, you'll always rebound. Upright and centered.

The second example is twirling. Have you ever watched a child make themselves dizzy by twirling around and around? Coming out of the spin, they either fall or stumble around trying to regain their footing.

Compare this with a professional ballet dancer who can do multiple pirouettes without getting dizzy. What's the difference? Training. They've learned what to do to keep from getting dizzy. That's what The Formula does—it trains you to focus your attention inward for balance.

God and the Ordinary

There are two other things for you to know.

When I speak about God, I mean God to be any name you give to your higher power. And if you don't have a higher power, that's fine, too.

I've had many spiritual mentors, wise beings, angels, and ancestors who've supported and given me guidance along my journey. I expect you have, too.

Start Chasing Nothing doesn't require you to align with any church, creed, or theology, and it isn't attached to any dogma, doctrine, or degree of attainment.

It's all good.

This book is written from the perspective of an ordinary woman living an ordinary life. Therefore, it's written for ordinary people going through their day with routines, responsibilities, and commitments. If you're looking for some magic tip or trick that will "poof" you out of your mundane life into extraordinary beingness, you'll be disappointed.

What you will find is a guide that will help you shift from suffering to peace, one second at a time.

Start Chasing Nothing

In this book, you'll read about the most common things ordinary people like us chase and why. You'll discover the number one reason people chase things and how you can use The Formula to stop chasing.

All within a loving, supportive environment.

No shame.

No blame.

We'll talk about happiness, too—how to be and stay happy. It's easier than you think once you Start. Chasing. Nothing.

I initially thought about naming this book "stop chasing something" or "stop chasing." And while it's true that you'll learn how to stop chasing, there's so much more to come once you've stopped the chase.

Step Three of The Formula is Shift.

Once you get beyond the chase, a world of infinite possibilities awaits you. No. I'm not exaggerating!

Stopping the chase is just the beginning.

Once it's stopped and your perspective has shifted, new insights and fresh opportunities will present themselves. Better connections will form, innovative ideas will come to you, and wisely chosen responses can be made.

Start Chasing Nothing is a guide for those who want to be happy—from the inside out:

> The Formula will show you how.
>
> The steps will make it easy.
>
> And your Emergency List (that you'll develop in chapter eight), will give you relief when you feel yourself spiraling downward into a quagmire of negativity.

If you're an ordinary person living an ordinary life, this book is for you.

If you're trying to figure out how to have deep, abiding happiness that is ever-present and lasting, this book will guide you.

If all you want is to be happier with your life, you'll be inspired by the stories of ordinary people just like you, who've discovered that their source of happiness flows from within.

Here's to your happiness!

PART I

THE FORMULA:
SEE
STOP AND BE STILL
SHIFT

Three simple steps that will profoundly impact your life.

CHAPTER 1

Waking Up

When the student is ready, the teacher will appear. ~ *Laozi*

I've been a chaser all my life.

As a child, I chased after my parents' approval by getting good grades and trying to be a "good girl." As a youth, it was all about my peers. So, I chased after ways to fit in and belong. As an adult, all I did was chase! I dangled the proverbial carrot on the end of a stick, and raced after degrees, qualifications, and career success. I married the "right" man, wore the "right" clothes, and behaved the "right" way.

It was exhausting!

Looking back, even I didn't like who I was.

Still, when you're seeking outside yourself for approval and struggling with not being good enough or feeling okay about yourself, chasing is what you do. You chase after things hoping they will make you happy.

The problem was, it was never enough. I always wanted more. As if a tapeworm had taken up residence in my stomach, I gobbled up each new attainment without ever feeling nourished.

If you're reading this book, I know you've experienced this too.

We all chase after things.

We're all in pain because of the chasing we do.

Until the cost of chasing becomes too much, and we start waking up.

Waking Up

We frequently hear about people having wake-up calls.

Shows depicting loved ones passing away, children mysteriously disappearing, and partners walking away are ubiquitous on television. I know people who've gone through career-ending disasters, catastrophic financial losses, and horrific religious persecution. Accidents, illnesses, and loss change everything.

Gradually Waking Up

My waking-up process was nothing so dramatic.

You see, I'd been in pain all my life—daily emotional distress was *normal* for me.

I had coped, carried on, and iron-willed my way through so many years of pain that chasing after something or someone external to me felt natural.

Time after time, I'd hoist up my big girl panties and charge on.

Without thinking, I'd race toward the next golden carrot, hoping that this would finally be the thing that would make me feel better.

I cringe thinking about how many times I ignored my inner voice urging me to look inward for happiness. Instead, I chased after the next "brass ring" on my interminable carousel ride.

Time to Pay the Piper

Eventually, the price of a lifetime of chasing caught up with me.

It was 2014.

For a couple of years, I'd known something was wrong.

At first, I noticed some unusual spotting between periods. I rationalized that my spotting was due to hormonal changes in my body.

Besides, I didn't have time to get it checked out. You know me. Busy. Chasing.

Later, as the bleeding increased, I was more annoyed than concerned. I was busy working and taking care of my family. Where could I possibly fit in an appointment to see a specialist? How inconvenient.

Finally, I couldn't ignore what was happening anymore. I was bleeding non-stop. When I went to see a doctor, my blood count was so dangerously low that I needed a blood transfusion!

In November, I was diagnosed with stage I-II uterine cancer and underwent a full hysterectomy. I was forty-two. My sons were fourteen and ten. It was an uncertain and scary time for all of us.

When the Student is Ready

After surgery, my doctor ordered me to stay home, rest, and recover. For someone who's been a chaser all her life, this could have been a jail sentence. Instead, it became a gift. A gift because, for the first time in my life, I got to focus entirely on myself. My health. My recovery. My wellness. I wasn't able to go to work or do much physical activity. My wonderful husband looked after our sons.

Time turned inward as the mantle of responsibility slipped from my shoulders.

Stillness entered as I pondered life.

"What's the meaning of life?"
"What's the point of all this?"

I asked. Listened. Then, asked some more. And with each asking, new doors opened, and books, programs, and teachers made themselves known to me. A deeper knowing settled in.

I knew I needed to let go of all the pain and suffering I'd accumulated from a lifetime of chasing. I drank up *Letting Go* by David R. Hawkins and almost all the books by Dr. Joseph Murphy.

One of the most influential books I read was *Autobiography of a Yogi* by Paramhansa Yogananda. I adore Yogananda! This book gave me hope that there's a world beyond and something bigger than myself on which to focus. This book, and *A Course in Miracles* by Helen Schucman, solidified my resolve to release the things I'd been chasing and go within to work on me. Ultimately, to be free and be love.

A Course in Miracles also helped me learn the real meaning of forgiveness, and to understand that judgments we make about people and things have no basis. They're illusions that mask our inner pain.

I read every book that Florence Scovel Shinn wrote and learned from her about the sacredness of thoughts and words. *Your Word Is Your Wand* is my favorite book about living life cheerfully. And *The Game of Life and How to Play It* helped me realize that I could manifest success and joy in everything I did.

The Surrender Experiment by Michael A. Singer taught me the importance of opening our hearts and surrendering to life and that everything is a gift from the universe.

From Abraham-Hicks I learned about vibrational frequency. What it is. How to raise it. And why you need to "let your cork rise."

The more I read, the more I learned. These books opened my eyes to new insights, greater knowing, and a fuller understanding of where I needed to go to end my suffering.

Within.

All that I read and all that I studied pointed in the same direction—everything starts from within.

So, I signed up for the Your Year of Miracles program and learned everything I could from mentors Debra Poneman, Marci Shimoff, Dr. Sue Morter, and Lisa Garr.

A year of mentoring under Debra Poneman gave me clarity and skills to live in the light of grace and true success.

It was becoming clear that nothing I had chased would, or could ever bring me lasting happiness.

Happiness is an inside job.

From the *Art of Living*, I learned how to experience deep, inner peace and discovered the joy of Sahaj Samadhi meditation. Through Sudarshan Kriya, I learned how to restore my natural rhythm of happiness. Deep insights poured into me, showered over me, and cleansed me from the inside out.

Within a year, I had completed my Executive Diploma in Corporate Coaching from Hong Kong University's SPACE Program and began coaching. It was time to start helping others.

The woman I was before, the one who relied on chasing for external recognition and things to keep me fulfilled, is not the woman I am today.

I am changed.

While I function quite well in the outer world, my true dwelling place is within. My inner world began changing the moment I accepted the invitation to awaken. And yours will also.

That Was Then—This Is Now!

At the beginning of this chapter, I quoted Chinese philosopher Laozi, "When the student is ready, the teacher will appear."

For me, there were many teachers. I'm grateful for them all.

Before 2014, I repetitively chased after external things and approval from others. I was angry most of the time and blamed others for how I felt. I was pessimistic and combative. At work, I was so competitive and aggressive that everyone avoided me. It was no fun being me or being around me.

Now, I'm more at peace. "She's more calm and less intense" is how my friends and family describe me.

I occasionally get triggered; however, I rarely lash out or blame others for my feelings or circumstances. And if I do, I catch myself right away.

I meditate every day. I'm a better friend, a more thoughtful mother, and a much kinder spouse. I listen more. Talk less. And four times a year, I go on silent retreats to still my mind.

Am I content? Yes.

Am I happy? I know how to be!

I use The Formula to make me happy.

Can you learn how to use The Formula to be happy, too?

Absolutely!

Your Time is Now

I wrote *Start Chasing Nothing* so you don't have to go through a life-threatening wake-up call. So you don't have to read lots of books, sign up for expensive programs, immerse yourself in weeklong silent retreats, or become certified in anything.

I wrote this book for you. To save you time, money, and ultimately, your life.

Of course, if you've already had a wake-up call, consider this book your lifeline. See me standing on the shore, throwing a lifebuoy your way. Grab a hold. It will keep you afloat while you find your footing.

You'll find your footing through a technique I've developed that will help you go within when waves are threatening to capsize you. It's called The Formula. Through it, you'll learn a new way to stabilize yourself and find inner peace quickly.

Start Chasing Nothing is for ordinary people who are dealing with prolonged daily dread, who chase after golden carrots desperately hoping to find acceptance and approval from something or someone other than yourself.

It's written for those searching for peace, longing for fulfillment, and needing a place to start.

I know the pain of chasing.

I know you do, too.

Start Chasing Nothing will help you navigate your way back home. Home to a more centered, peaceful place.

What You Can Expect

I don't hold back.

You'll see warts and healing—failures, mistakes, and growth. In the "My Story" sections, you'll witness The Formula in action, and the steps I use to go from red-hot emotions to calm, cool center.

Scattered throughout the book are personal examples of the chasing I've done. You'll read about what I've done wrong and what I wish I did differently. You'll weep with me at my shortcomings, and cheer me on as I make headway.

You'll laugh with me and be surprised at my honesty—"I can't believe she said that!" And you will see for yourself how everyday moments really *can* be profound learning opportunities.

Part I of *Start Chasing Nothing* is the core of my teaching. In it, you'll learn about The Formula.

There are three steps in The Formula—very easy steps—that anyone can do. They are:

1. See
2. Stop and Be Still
3. Shift

I'll guide you through each step, give you plenty of examples of what they look like in action, and provide you with the opportunity to try them out for yourself.

At the end of **Part I**, I talk about the Emergency List. I explain how it came into existence and what a lifesaver it was (and still is) at work, home, and everywhere else. I consider this to be the best thing I've ever done for myself! To this day, I still use my Emergency List whenever I feel the least bit off-center.

You'll see my Emergency List, and I'll help you develop one for yourself. That way, you'll be ready any time you need to extinguish your red-hot emotions or snuff them out before they engulf you.

All of **Part III** is devoted to things you can do right now to stop yourself from focusing on the mind stories, return to center, and take control of yourself.

Here you'll find everyday applications of The Formula that will help you out in various situations, from dealing with the Monday Blues to using meditation to still your mind.

I share calming techniques like Dr. Sue Morter's Central Channel Breathing when you need to ground yourself, and One Second at a Time when you need to restore your sanity—I use that one a lot!

Near the end of the book, I share a very special message for parents and show you how the whole family can incorporate the

Hawaiian practice of Ho'oponopono for Reconciliation and Forgiveness.

In between Part I and III is the heart of *Start Chasing Nothing*. **Part II** discusses the six main things we all chase:

1. Approval
2. Control of others
3. The past
4. Façades
5. Success
6. Money

At the beginning of each chapter, I lay the foundation by explaining what it means to chase. Each chapter has a "My Story" so you can see examples of how I've chased. And you'll realize what the cost of chasing extracted from me. I lay it all out there so you can see how it impacted me and those around me.

I also share lots of uplifting examples of what other people have gained from stopping the chase, how their lives were transformed as they started chasing nothing, and what they learned along their journey. Their stories will touch you, and their words of wisdom will inspire you!

At the end of each chapter, there's a "Your Turn" section. Here, you'll have the opportunity to journal about what you've just learned, and to discover more about who you are, and discern who you'd like to become. As you let go of what you've been chasing and embrace being you, lasting happiness will emerge.

Finally, at the back of the book is an extensive resource section where I've included everything I've read, listened to, and tried that worked for me. You'll find books, programs, techniques, and websites that I currently use or have used in the past. All were helpful to me along my journey.

Skim this book for tips and techniques. Better yet, devour *Start Chasing Nothing* to free yourself from whatever you're chasing so you can be happy, no matter your current circumstance.

The student is ready.

I'm here, cheering you on!

CHAPTER 2

Ordinary Woman

Be content with an ordinary life. ~ Laozi

I'm an ordinary woman, living an ordinary life, with an ordinary job, who happened to figure out three simple steps to restore sanity and peace, one second at a time.

These three steps aren't anything new. You'll find parts of these steps scattered around in techniques used by other people. However, I've put them together in a powerful and meaningful way that helped me have and live a happy life, and I believe it will do the same for you.

In 2018, I began developing The Formula because I was on a do-or-die mission to figure out what I needed to do to be happy.

I had two wonderful sons, a fabulous husband, marvelous friends, a job that I liked, and enough money to be comfortable. But I wasn't happy.

What was wrong with me?

I took ski trips to Japan, traveled to India for retreats and to the United States for events.

Why wasn't I happy?

That was the driving question from which The Formula and Emergency List sprung. While I developed The Formula for myself, so many people saw what a difference it made in my life that they wanted to use it, too.

As a result, *Start Chasing Nothing* came into being. It's my way of giving hope to all ordinary women who also want to be happy.

Ordinary Life

Like most people, I get up every day and commute to and from work. When I get home, I'm exhausted. I have dinner, spend time with my family, go to sleep and start the next day pretty much like any other day.

I get a paycheck every month. I pay the bills with what I earn. I look forward to the weekends, time off, holidays, and spending time with my family.

I shop for groceries, visit with friends, try to eat healthfully, and exercise regularly.

I have an ordinary life, like you.

The Hero's Journey—For Women, Too

The Hero's Journey is a monomyth — a standard template of stories that involves a hero who goes on an adventure, 'slaying dragons, and returns home changed or transformed. Monomyth narratives are found worldwide.

American mythologist, Dr. Joseph Campbell devoted his life to researching the Hero's Journey, and he found it a myth of such great importance that it's included in all the major world cultures. With their mythological and religious heroes (Osiris, Prometheus, Moses, and Buddha, to name a few), these myths and their heroes have survived for thousands of years. And all share the same fundamental structure.

Although the stages or steps along the journey vary, the three main aspects of the Hero's Journey remain the same:

- Departure
- Initiation
- Return

The adventure begins when the hero, or in my case, heroine, receives a call to action. She is "drawn into a relationship with forces that are not rightly understood."[1]

After the heroine has accepted the call and sets off on her journey, she must cross the threshold between the world with which she is familiar to the unknown. And it's upon this road of trials that the heroine is tested, honed, and strengthened by the journey.

The last part of the Heroine's Journey is the return home. Before returning home, however, there is usually some sacrifice required—something the heroine must willingly leave behind. The sacrifice is always some part of the heroine that needs transforming.

My Heroine's Story

Departure—My call to action was to figure out how to be happy!

No, not the fleeting happiness that comes and goes, but the deep abiding happiness that is ever-present and lasting.

I wanted that kind of happiness.

I know it sounds like a cliché—I just wanted to be happy—however, as you know from reading the preface, I was in dire straits. Every. Single. Day. I awoke with debilitating dread and called out to God for help getting out of bed. I was depressed and anxious. On many occasions, my throat constricted so much, I could hardly breathe.

For no reason I could figure out, I was dreadfully unhappy.

This is no way to live—for anyone!

I've lost count of the numerous techniques and therapies I tried to help me with my unhappiness. None of them brought lasting relief. While some were helpful, each day continued to be a struggle and they didn't offer the lasting outcome I was seeking.

I just had to figure this out!

Initiation

It's this resolve and determination that started me on my Heroine's Journey and sustained me as I crossed the threshold from a world of despair to an unknown world of happiness.

At the start of the journey, I had no idea what it would be like to enter a world of happiness. I didn't even know what lasting happiness felt like yet alone where to find it. I just knew that I had to find it. And I was willing to be changed in the process.

I began by adjusting my attitude.

While I still went through the same daily routine, I altered my attitude. Instead of feeling downtrodden, I felt grateful. (Going through my day with gratitude in my heart is what helped me become happy.) Whenever I caught myself thinking negatively about someone or something, I blessed and thanked them instead.

Next, I changed how I dealt with sadness. Now when I felt sad, for whatever reason, instead of allowing it to overtake me, I turned to my Emergency List (more about this in chapter eight) and did the things there that would center me, calm me, and help me stop my twirling and turn inward for balance and peace.

I did this every day, every waking moment, for months. No. I'm not exaggerating.

In addition, I began monitoring my body like a hawk. Whenever I felt my body tense, stomach clench, or throat contract, I immediately pulled out my Emergency List instead of grinning and bearing it.

Slowly, my perspective shifted, and my life changed. While I was the same person on the outside, on the inside, things were changing. I felt happier. The dread began lifting, the anxiety lessened, and my overall outlook improved.

Energetically, I showed up differently and attracted more positive people and experiences. People were nicer to me, and I to them. I was more approachable and more willing to engage with others. The universe responded by sending me new, supportive friends to walk with me on my journey. And lots of ordinary people to coach and help on their Heroine's Journey to find inner happiness.

This was when I knew that The Formula worked. Not only did it work for me, but it also worked for everyone I coached.

For the first time in decades, I truly felt happy and at peace.

I knew that *I had the power* to make myself happy. To be happy and at peace wherever I was, whatever was going on, and whenever I wanted.

This was my aha moment—and I can't tell you what a liberating revelation this was for me!

When people ask me how The Formula came into being, it was from this crucible of pain that The Formula was borne:

> I was at my wit's end, and I had reached the point where I could no longer go on with the way things were. Something needed to change.

Return

Now, it was time to return home. A sacrifice was required. Something I was willing to leave behind—it was the part that needed transforming.

What was it, you wonder?

I think you know—I dropped all reliance on external people and things to make me happy.

What's Changed?

My happiness.

As a result of my Hero's/Heroine's Journey, I have learned to find fulfillment within. I have a deep knowing that all is well.

The journey that created The Formula was one of self-discovery. It was about finding life's joy and peace from within me rather than outside of me.

I'm the leading lady in my show. I no longer let anyone or anything steal my spotlight. Through a combination of meditation and intention to live in a more aware and meaningful way, my life is full of joy and peace. And I can honestly say that I love my life.

I use my Emergency List daily.

I no longer chase someone or something outside of me in the hope of finding lasting happiness. Instead, I work The Formula and go inward to discover the source from which all happiness flows.

Does that mean I'm happy all the time?

No.

Just like you, there are things that irritate and upset me. And I have ups and downs in my day. After all, I'm an ordinary woman living an ordinary life. The difference is, I have The Formula and know what to do to quickly switch from unhappy to happy.

Ordinary People Book

Start Chasing Nothing is an ordinary book written for ordinary people living ordinary lives who want to find lasting happiness.

It doesn't matter what religious affiliation you belong to, who or what you believe in, or even if you don't. The Formula isn't attached to any dogma, doctrines, or degrees of attainment.

It doesn't matter if you have a little money or a lot. It doesn't matter if you're climbing the career ladder or comfortable where you are. It doesn't matter if your life is ordinary or extraordinary. The only thing you need is a desire to attain lasting inner peace and fulfillment.

This book is a practical guide that helps you shift from suffering to peace one second at a time.

It's simple—three steps.

It's easy—use it any time you need relief from the drama swirling around you.

It's transformative—the techniques will help you calm what disturbs you and return you to your inner source of wisdom and strength.

Start Chasing Nothing includes the very same tools I used on my journey. You'll learn how to use The Formula and Emergency List to help you be happy from the inside out, so you can stop chasing outside factors to do it for you.

If I can do it, you can do it too—we're on this Hero's/Heroine's Journey together.

CHAPTER 3

Shift of Consciousness

The pain pushes until the vision pulls. ~ *Michael Beckwith*

Are you sick and tired of being sick and tired? Many people aren't, you know. They like being a part of the drama; they cling to blame and even relish playing the role of the victim—although they'd never admit it to anyone, even to themselves.

That's how it was with me.

I was in pain.

I was addicted to chasing pain.

Until I wasn't.

If you're reading this book, I know you're sick and tired of the drama, the blame, and feeling like a victim.

This is a great place to be, dear reader!

It means you're ready for a shift of consciousness.

Shift Your Consciousness

What does that even mean?

Given the enormous difficulty of even defining consciousness, here is an easy definition that will suit our purposes: A shift of consciousness is a change in perception that results in a greater awareness of behavior.

Rumi, the thirteenth-century poet and Sufi mystic, describes the shift of consciousness beautifully:

When I run after what I think I want,
My days are a furnace of distress and anxiety.
If I sit in my own place of patience,
What I need flows to me,
And without any pain.

From this, I understand that
What I want also wants me,
Is looking for me and attracting me;
When it cannot attract me
Any more to go to it,
It has come to me.
There's a great secret
In this for anyone who can grasp it.[1]

What Happens When Consciousness Shifts?

The first thing you'll notice is a letting go of the aggression and anger you once clung to. You'll quit blaming others and stop relying on them for happiness. Instead of living in a mental mind field exploding with worry, doubt, fear, and limitation, you'll discover an inner landscape of peace.

You'll start taking responsibility for your life, own how you feel, and begin forgiving yourself and others.

You'll become kinder and more loving. You'll feel compassion for others, and see them without the lens of judgment or attachment.

As a result, you'll naturally pull away from toxic people and shed destructive habits. Drama will no longer appeal to you, as it will no longer feed or sustain you.

Comparing yourself to others and competing with them won't make sense anymore. Support will replace competitiveness.

You now understand that by helping others, you're helping yourself.

When you shift to a higher level of consciousness, how you view and understand life changes.

Gratitude and appreciation are now the hallmarks of who and how you are in the world. You see the good in yourself and others. You appreciate all you currently have in life, and the things you'll have in the future.

You have a deep knowing that we're all connected. Not only do you understand it intellectually, but you'll also feel it deeply.

This is true freedom. Inner-peace freedom. "The peace of God that passes all understanding."[2]

Raise Your Vibration

"Yeah, but..." I can hear you saying, "That all sounds well and good, but let's get real. I live in a practical world. What's all this talk about raising vibrations?"

I used to wonder the same thing.

Been there. Thought that!

Here's what I now know—the key to shifting your consciousness is to raise your vibrational frequency.

Everything Vibrates

The law of nature states that everything has its own vibration. Or, as theoretical physicist Albert Einstein says, "Everything in life is vibration."

The universe consists of molecules vibrating at different speeds. Some molecules vibrate faster, and some slower, which means higher and lower vibrational frequencies.

If your molecules are moving faster, then you're vibrating at a higher frequency. Your energy is lighter. You'll feel happier and more at ease.

You experience greater personal power, more clarity, peace, love, and joy! Your life flows with synchronicity, and you manifest what you desire with ease.

When your molecules are moving slowly, you're vibrating at a lower frequency. Your energy is denser. You'll feel heavy, dark, and sluggish. Your problems feel weighty. Accomplishing goals takes a great deal of effort.

Esther Hicks, who channels Abraham, points out, "As you think, you vibrate. As you vibrate, you attract."

So, lighten up, dear reader!

The point of shifting consciousness is to keep your vibration high and light.

The Formula

Let me introduce you to a technique I've developed that will help you shift your consciousness and raise your vibrational frequency.

I call it, The Formula. And I want you to think about it as your personal fire extinguisher.

It's a simple yet powerful practice that quickly turns your "furnace of distress and anxiety" into a place of calm and peace.

In the following chapters, I'll explain how The Formula works, show you my Emergency List and help you develop yours, and share real-life examples of how I've used The Formula in my own life.

You can use it anytime, from the moment you feel even the slightest bit off-center, to when you're full-on raging mad. No matter what degree of stress or anxiety you're experiencing, The Formula will help you still your mind and calm yourself into a place of inner peace.

The Formula works!

Let's talk more about The Formula.

CHAPTER 4

The Formula

You realize something very extraordinary is happening here:
There are no ordinary moments in your life. ~ Mary O'Malley

As you know, I have been a chaser all my life.

First, as a young child trying to please my parents, then as a youth wanting desperately to fit in. As I got older, it just got worse. I chased after degrees, accomplishments, and status symbols. I went to the "right" schools, married the "right" man, made sure that I lived in a lovely home, had two wonderful sons...and was miserable.

I spent nearly four decades searching for happiness in all the wrong places.

I woke up every day, dreading the start of my day and begging God for help. My throat would constrict to such a degree that I had difficulty breathing. Even on ski holidays with my family, I couldn't relax. I was the hamster in the wheel, and the way I dealt with it was by becoming hyper-controlling.

You've heard of the phrase "tiger mom," haven't you? It was coined in Amy Chua's book, *The Battle Hymn of the Tiger Mother,* and is associated with a type of parenting style commonly associated with mothers who are strict and demanding. Yep. That was me.

Also known as a control freak, I tried to control everyone and everything.

As things spiraled downward in my life, I doubled down on controlling even more. I was constantly stressed, peevish, and snippy with colleagues and friends. No one lived up to my standards, especially me. I was no fun to be around and didn't have much joy in my life.

Then, at the age of forty-two, I was diagnosed with the "Big C" and underwent a full hysterectomy. While I'm not saying that being a chaser and trying to control everything *caused* my cancer, I am saying that it contributed significantly to it.

Uterine cancer was my wake-up call and the beginning of my journey from a hyper-controlling, tiger-mom-chaser to an in-the-moment, present-centered woman.

Overview of The Formula

Do you remember the Weeble? That roly-poly egg-shaped toy that Hasbro introduced in 1971. Weebles came in varying shapes and sizes; however, what they all had in common was a weighted bottom that, when punched, kicked, or hit, always bounced back to their upright position. My boys enjoyed playing with one as children and never tired of trying to get the best of their Weeble. Still, no matter what they did or how hard they tried, the Weeble always rebounded. Upright and centered.

"Weebles wobble, but they don't fall down."

That's what The Formula will do for you. It will help you get back up, no matter what punch you've taken.

Complementary to Other Practices

One of the things that's great about The Formula is that although it's different from other popular self-help practices, it doesn't exclude other techniques; however, it can be used in conjunction with them.

For instance, some people have compared The Formula to Byron Katie's *The Work*. I'm a big admirer of Byron Katie and recommend her technique when you need to examine what's true and untrue about your thoughts and beliefs.

The Formula doesn't question your thoughts or beliefs. Instead, it redirects attention from your mind to your body. That's because your mind often focuses on the past and the future instead of the present. In contrast, your body resides entirely in the present. It's about the present moment and what's happening now.

Instead of focusing on thought patterns in your mind, The Formula moves you into feeling sensations within your body. Like the Weeble, this process will anchor you from within and help you bounce back to the center.

I think the Formula is similar to Eckhart Tolle's method of focusing on the now and the Sedona Method, which focuses on the release of sensations. But the difference is that The Formula doesn't require any analysis for it to work.

I've found that putting attention on your mind and what you're thinking when you're hurting is comparable to pouring gasoline onto a fire—kaboom!

The Formula trains you to reach for the Emergency List like you would use the fire extinguisher the moment you see smoke. That way, you can extinguish the emotional fire and make calm, response-able decisions rather than raging emotional reactions.

The Greyhound and the Rabbit

As you use The Formula, you will begin to see that it is your thoughts that cause your emotional turmoil. This reminds me of this story that my friend Susan shared with me about greyhound racing dogs in North America.

Up until a few years ago, greyhound racing dogs were euthanized when they got too old to race or too old for breeding. For those unfamiliar with greyhound racing, it's an organized, competitive sport, much like horse racing, except the dogs chase a rabbit around the track.

Feeling sorry for the dogs, a group of ladies started an adoption agency in Florida whose sole purpose was to find "forever homes" for these beautiful athletes.[1] Sally was one of their first customers. She fell in love with and quickly adopted Gus.

That Thanksgiving, Sally's father came for a visit. After dinner, he went to visit Gus in the backyard. Affectionately rubbing his ears, he asked:

> "Gus, how are you doing?"
>
> "Life is good! I have a big yard to play in, two meals a day, and an owner who loves me."
>
> "Did you ever race? Did you ever win?"
>
> "Yes, I did and won five times!"
>
> "Really! How come you're not running anymore? Did you get too old?"
>
> "No, I quit."
>
> "Why did you quit?"
>
> Gus leaned in closer and whispered, "I found out the rabbit wasn't real."

Dear reader, as you adopt The Formula as your own, you'll come to understand that the thoughts inside your head aren't real.

As Gurudev Sri Sri Ravi Shankar says, "Once you know that it is your own mind that is bothering you, and not somebody else, then wisdom dawns!"

Step One Crib Sheet
See

To See means to become aware of the emotional fire within you. You can't put out the flames until you See and identify what the fire is, and where it's living within your body.

This book is intended to be read in its entirety before applying The Formula; however, once you understand the process, use the crib sheets at the beginning of each relevant chapter as a quick reference guide.

CHAPTER 5

Step One—See

Because you've been down there, Neo. You know where that road ends.
And I know that's not where you want to be. ~ The Matrix

Everyone knows what it's like to have a bad day.

Remember that scene in *The Matrix* when Agent Smith is interrogating Neo? He's in trouble. His double life as Thomas A. Anderson, program writer for a respectable software company and computer hacker, Neo searching for Morpheus, is exposed. Neo refuses to cooperate with Agent Smith, his lips creepily fuse together, and a robotic tracking bug burrows into his body. Neo is having a *really* bad day!

The next time you see Neo, he's waiting under the Adam Street Bridge. A car pulls up with Trinity, Apoc, and Switch inside. Switch opens the door and commands:

> "Get in."
> "What the hell is this?"
> "Right now, there's only one rule: Our way or the highway."
> Neo reaches for the door handle to get out of the car. "Fine."
> Trinity stops him. "Please, Neo. You have to trust me."
> "Why?"
> "Because you've been down there, Neo. You know where that road ends. And I know that's not where you want to be."

Neo is at a crossroads. He pauses to See the situation. If he gets out of the car, nothing will change. If he remains in the car, he'll have the opportunity for something better.

That's the first step of The Formula—See the situation. See what you're experiencing

My Story

As you know, most of my life, I'd wake up in the morning feeling anxious and sick to my stomach. Every morning— no, I'm not exaggerating—I cried out to God, "Help me get up!" At work, my throat tightened up, my chest constricted, and my muscles clenched. I couldn't breathe!
Worst of all, I didn't know why.
What was the problem!
And so, my mind went into overdrive, trying to figure out why this was happening. It sifted through memories, looking for someone to blame. It focused on the situation, giving me something to complain about or someone to hold responsible. When that didn't work, it tried to remedy the situation by having me purchase more clothes, eat more food, and go on more holidays.
Then came the ski trip I talked about in the preface when I realized what was happening to me, and therefore, what could help me, wasn't external to me. The answers were within.

I now know that negative "stuff"—I know, very scientific of me— happens in everyone's life. Your body experiences it first and reacts by contracting. Then, your mind quickly engages by searching your conscious mind, where thoughts and memories within your awareness are stored.

When nothing can be found, it searches your unconscious where past events and buried memories are stockpiled.

Once your body experiences "stuff," your body reacts, and your mind starts searching. And since the body is in the present and the mind is in the past, your mind has to search in the conscious (near) and unconscious (distant) past for a time when something similar happened. It does this so it can inform your present self on how to proceed.

So, What's the Problem?

That's a great question.

Here's the answer—hang in here with me, dear reader—When your mind starts searching around in the past for answers as to why your body has contracted, it's looking for a similar experience. When it finds it, or multiple related events, it informs your present self that what's occurring is "another one of those unhappy experiences."

Wait. What?

Clear as mud?

Let's look at this from a different perspective.

You see, when your body feels uneasy (contracted), your mind searches for a time in the past when something similar happened. It then makes up a story to rationalize what's happening within the body. In other words, it extrapolates from the past to inform the present and predict the future.

Wowzah!

Looping

Remember the 1993 movie *Groundhog Day* starring Bill Murray? He plays a cynical weatherman, Phil Conner, trapped in a time loop, forced to relive the same day, over and over.

Groundhog Day has become such a pop-culture touchstone that it's frequently referenced when someone's stuck in a rut and repeating the same pattern.

"Insanity is doing the same thing over and over again but expecting different results." So said fictional character Jane Fulton in Rita May Brown's book, *Sudden Death*.

Whether it's an argument that keeps coming up, tiresome nagging about the same thing, or blame that never gets resolved, it's all looping.

When your mind starts looping, it's a problem.

That's why you can't expect your mind to solve your present-day problem when it's your mind that's creating a "Groundhog Day" with the past.

If you want to stay stuck in a rut, keep thinking the same thoughts.

If you want the opportunity for something better, do what Neo did—See the situation.

Your Body Is Your Friend

Once you See the situation and what you're experiencing, next, close your eyes and check in with your body. Feel around. Scan the different spaces within you.

No judgment. Just be.

Scan the area around your heart, within your belly, and the space about your throat. Scan your head for any tension there.

Now, direct your attention to the area within your body where you sense the most significant contraction. See it. Feel it. Then, take a breath and breathe through the contracted energy to release and dissipate throughout your system.

Take a breath and do it again.

Breathe through the contraction as long as needed to feel a release.

It's perfectly natural as you're releasing contracted and stored energy for deep emotions to emerge. It's okay to cry, sob, shout, groan, or sigh. Whatever emotion comes up is okay to express.

Let your emotions surface.

No judgment. Just be.

Releasing the stuck energy is what's needed to get fresh energy flowing through your body.

Your body is your friend because only your body can release the energy that is stuck there.

In Marci Shimoff's book, *Happy for No Reason*, she explains the two types of sensations—contraction and expansion.

> "When you feel positive emotions like happiness, joy, and enthusiasm, your body feels expansive. When you experience negative feelings, like anger, jealousy, and pain, your body feels contracted.[1]"

The more you practice going within and feeling around for contracted energy places, the easier it will get.

The more you breathe into these contracted areas, the lighter you'll become.

The Mind-Body Connection

The mind and body are not two separate entities, although they're often treated that way. What we think and how we feel are intimately entwined.

Have you ever noticed that when you feel happy, you have more energy to do things? And when you feel sad, all you want to do is lie in bed all day.

Our mind-body connection is a two-way stream. What's experienced within the body is linked to how the mind interprets the experience. Conversely, our thoughts can influence how we feel in the body.

As author Mike Dooley puts it, "Thoughts become things."

If what you're thinking about causes you to feel angry, your body will reflect this anger by contracting. And if what you're thinking about brings you happiness, your body responds by expanding.

The mind affects the body, and the body affects the mind.

Release and Affirm

The final thing to do is release the negative energy trapped within your body and affirm what you want to create.

Releasing and affirming is my favorite part of this step. And I've come to know that the more I release contracted, stored energy, the more differently I view the world. Once I See the situation for what it is, I no longer view "problems" the same way. I no longer view people as adversarial.

When stuff comes up, and it still does for me, I turn to The Formula to help me See, feel, flow, and release. It's the way I stop the habitual *Groundhog Day* loop. It's how I get myself into a better feeling state, Shift consciousness, and raise my vibrational frequency to a lighter, more clear state of being. It is in this state that I can see more clearly.

Here are some of my favorite affirmations which I use to clear away the dark clouds over my head:

> "I release all negative energy and welcome in peace."
> "I am releasing what no longer serves me, and expanding into my highest potential."
> "I release negative energy into love and light, and I go free."

Feel free to use these or one of your own.

Now, you can see clearly, too!

Helpful Tip

If you're Seeing the situation and what you're experiencing, and you're yet finding it difficult to untangle from the drama, here's a technique that will help you gain perspective.

Yell, "Cut!"

Imagine yourself sitting in a movie theater, watching a great film. You're so involved with the drama of the movie that you get lost in it.

I know. It happens to me all the time!

You and the actor are one. The actor's body tenses. Your body tenses. Their heart races and yours does, too. Your eyes well up at tearful good-byes and marriages of star-crossed lovers. You're all in.

"Cut!"

Now, move yourself to the *balcony* of the movie theater. You're no longer a part of the action or caught up in the drama.

You're *observing* the movie, much like a film director does. The director sits in the balcony to gain perspective and objectivity. This is what you want to have, also.

So, the next time you're caught up in the drama of stuff and are having trouble untangling from the emotions of the situation, yell, "Cut!" And chop the air as if you're holding the clapperboard that ends the scene.

Yell "Cut!" and slam the clapperboard to end the drama as many times as needed. I know, it sounds funny. And feels funny, too. But it works!

It cuts the scene and allows you to put yourself in the director's chair. It will enable you to step back from and out of the drama, so you can observe what you're feeling within your body.

> *When you are present in this moment, you break the continuity of your story, of past and future. Then true intelligence arises, and also love.* ~ Eckhart Tolle

Step Two Crib Sheet

Stop and Be Still

To Stop and Be Still means stopping yourself from focusing on the mind stories. Then Be Still and surrender to what you're feeling.

Remember; your mind recalls the past and projects into the future while your body resides in the present moment. Therefore, Stop and Be Still to prevent your mind from engaging with past stories or future worries. It's about interrupting your attention on the mind stories so that you can Stop and Be Still in the present moment.

Once you've done that, check in with your body and sense where there's contracted energy. Follow the sensation and identify where it is in your body. Recognize how you're feeling, acknowledge the feeling, then release it by breathing into it, so your energy flows more freely.

While you're doing this, make no judgments. Instead, say, "I'm okay. Everything's okay. I trust that all is well."

This book is intended to be read in its entirety before applying The Formula; however, once you understand the process, use the crib sheets at the beginning of each relevant chapter as a quick reference guide.

CHAPTER 6

Step Two—Stop and Be Still

When you lose touch with inner stillness, you lose touch with yourself.
When you lose touch with yourself, you lose yourself in the world."
~ Eckhart Tolle

Tom Cronin's world was falling apart.

He was so overwhelmed and so overridden with anxiety that he couldn't even walk out the front door of his apartment. He was crashing physically, mentally, and emotionally. He literally couldn't function.

He was no longer able to handle the pressures of a culture that defined success to be all about chasing more. More money. More power. More extravagance.

In 2013 he founded *The Stillness Project* and has this to say about what brought him to this change of life and career:

> "In 1987 I landed a job on a trading room floor as a broker, trading bonds for the investment banks. It was fast; there was lots of adrenaline. I was making a ton of money.
> As a result of the stress and some very poor lifestyle choices, I suffered these extreme panic attacks and depression. There was this heavy dark cloud that hung over my head every day. I'd lost interest in everything and felt checked out of life.

In the process, I discovered Eastern philosophy and meditation. Everything I'd been looking for in my life I was finding here in this place of stillness. Very quickly, the anxiety and depression floated away. I felt this lightness and calm and happiness.

Now, I travel worldwide, teaching people how to unlock their brilliance and inner stillness with meditation.[1]"

Stillness is powerful.

Not only does it reduce stress, but it also cultivates peace, calms emotions, and stabilizes you from the inside out. As Laozi says, "When there is silence, one finds the anchor of the universe within oneself."

My Story

Before my "aha moment," my life had become an endless string of bad days. I wondered, more than once, if something was seriously wrong with me.

The life I was living and the path I had taken had me continually chasing after the wrong things in life. And the more I chased, the more I needed to chase.

My life had become an endless loop going nowhere.

Your Story

So, what's your story?

Do you see a little of me in you? Perhaps your life is crashing down around you as it did with Tom.

Take a few moments to think about your life and where you are now. See the situation and what you've experienced. Stop yourself from focusing on the mind stories. Then Be Still and surrender to what you're feeling.

Now ask yourself, "How did I get here?"

Examine what you're experiencing within your body.

After you've thought about it, take a moment to write your story down. You can either take out your journal and write about it or pen it here in this book:

_____

_____

_____

_____

_____

_____

_____

_____

_____

_____

_____

_____

Next, ask yourself this basic question: "Am I ready for a change?"

_____

My Story

If you'd asked me that question before my "aha" moment, I would have said, "No. I'm good. I'll figure it out. I'll just do more!"

After my "aha" moment, it was a resounding "Yes." My life depended on it!

However, I must tell you, dear reader, that while I knew I needed to change, it didn't happen overnight. In actuality, it was a "baby step" journey for me.

> In the most intense situations—when I was in dire help-lessness and my mind was in chaos, I'd Stop and tell myself, "Just focus on this one second, Elaine. Don't focus on anything else but this one second."
>
> Then I'd feel it—that place of inner stillness. For one second, I knew I was okay. I felt safe. I was anchored. And if I could calm my mind and find inner stillness for one second, I could do it for five seconds. Then 15 seconds. Finally, 60 seconds!
>
> For one minute, I felt relief from the pain that had consumed me for most of my life—the pain of not feeling good enough that made me want to chase more.

I realize how lame it must seem that I celebrated one second of stillness. Yet, for me, it was a big deal. Because that's when I finally "got it" that the way out from my misery wasn't to focus *outward* by finding ways to do more. It was to Stop focusing on the crazy-making mind stories. Then Be Still and surrender to whatever I was feeling. Focus *inward* on the stillness within me.

Tom crashed physically, mentally, and emotionally.

I asked God for help each morning getting out of bed.

What about you?

If your mind is incessantly churning and your emotions relentlessly roiling, wouldn't one second of stillness feel amazing?

What about one minute?

A day?

The relief is indescribable!

If it feels as if your life is spinning out of control and you've reached the end of your rope, then I'll ask you this basic question: "Are you ready for a change?"

Stop

Tom Cronin realized that "everything he'd been looking for in his life was this place of stillness." I figured out that first, you must Stop yourself from focusing on the mind stories.

Before you can go inward and experience stillness, See the situation for what it is and Stop what you're doing. Stop focusing on the crazy-making mind stories.

In the previous chapter, you learned how to get out of the drama by visualizing yourself in the movie theater's balcony, *watching* the movie instead of being *in* the movie. Getting out of the film's drama and into the seat as an observing director helps you gain perspective.

So how do you Stop?

A fun way to visualize this is by seeing yourself at the top of a long playground slide. It's your turn—whee!

But, instead of sliding to the bottom, squeeze with your hands and Stop your momentum. Midway down, physically Stop yourself from sliding.

Stop.

Now, you're ready to go inward and experience the power of stillness.

Be Still

Once you've physically Stopped, now it's time to take your attention off what's going on around you. Stop analyzing the problem. Stop trying to come up with a solution or predict what's going to happen.

Be Still and surrender to what you're feeling.

Get out of your mind.

Quiet your body.

Find a restful place where you can sit peacefully. It could be in a garden on a park bench, in your office with the door closed, or at home in your sacred space. It doesn't matter where you are. It just needs to be a place where you can quiet your body and Be Still in your mind. (When you've done this many times, it becomes much easier to Be Still in your mind, even when you're in activity.)

Next, direct your attention to the place within you that's calm, like a tranquil body of water where you can float effortlessly. A place of solitude. A place of peace.

Here is where you'll find stillness—the place where your mind has surrendered to the peace of your soul, where you feel nothing *and* you feel everything. The in-between place where you understand what Byron Katie means when she says, "All I have is all I need, and all I need is all I have in this moment."

You feel and experience silence. You are peaceful and are peace itself. Same with joy, bliss, and true happiness. Words can't adequately describe this in-between place because you're no longer in your mind. You're abiding in the seat of your soul.

At first, you may only be able to get there and experience stillness for one second. That's perfectly fine. Even good, because you *did* manage to Stop and Be Still. Then, like me, if you can do it for one second, you can do it for five seconds and even longer!

As you rest in this place of stillness, it's perfectly natural for thoughts to form and vie for your attention. That's okay. Just observe the thoughts as they come up. And see them pass by, as if you are lying on your back and watching the clouds pass by.

See your thoughts but don't latch onto them. No need to ponder or ruminate. Instead, watch them pass by, as if you're driving in a car, seeing road signs pass by without taking any notice.

Feel the expansiveness of the place within you. Feel how calm it is and how it "anchors you to the universe within yourself." Here is where intuition resides, where insights dwell and answers are revealed.

Here, in this stillness, is where you'll get in touch with and become attuned to your inner being. And from this place, right action springs forth. This simple act of Stopping and Being Still is what Shifts you into a higher state of consciousness and raises your vibrational frequency.

The basis for all change is through the individual experience of stillness. - Tom Cronin

Step Three Crib Sheet

Shift

To Shift means to begin climbing up the vibrational ladder to a place of higher frequency vibration, to a place of joy and positivity where you're focused and happy.

The Shift to climb up the vibration ladder differs depending on the person as well as the situation. That's why having an Emergency List is so helpful!

One of the first things you'll notice is that you're reacting less to what initially upset you. And you're feeling more kindhearted towards others and gentle with yourself.

Soon, you'll feel within your body the sensations of expansion and openness. You'll release and go with the flow, rather than resisting and pushing against things.

Sometimes, the Shift is made possible through gratitude. Other times, through love.

Shifting through gratitude is very powerful because when you focus on what you're grateful for in life, your attention organically Shifts from what upsets you to what makes you feel happy.

Shifting through love is tremendously healing because it can include forgiveness— for others and for yourself. If you're in a situation where you're distressed by what someone has done, it may be forgiveness that will take you up the ladder so you can Shift to a higher vibration.

Now that you've Shifted to a new vantage point, new insights and fresh opportunities will present themselves, and wisely chosen responses can be made.

This book is intended to be read in its entirety before applying The Formula; however, once you understand the process, use the crib sheets at the beginning of each relevant chapter as a quick reference guide.

CHAPTER 7

Step Three—Shift

When you shift your consciousness, you shift your reality.
~ *Syed Sharukh*

There's an old Chinese Proverb that discerns, "When the winds of change blow, some people build walls and others build windmills."

The windmill is a fantastic metaphor for this final step in The Formula.

When you look at a windmill, what do you see?

Of course, you see the movement of the blades. And you understand that it's from this movement that wind energy converts into power, a power that can be converted into electricity and used for grinding grain and pumping water.

You can't help but admire a windmill's enormous transformational power!

Much as a windmill converts wind energy into electricity, a Shift of consciousness has the transformational power to convert your current situation into a higher vibrational frequency.

What a Shift of Consciousness Will Do for You

In the Native American tradition, there are four spirit keepers of the Medicine Wheel: eagle, buffalo, bear, and mouse.

The eagle stands for wisdom. As a totem animal, eagle represents the ability to see higher, broader truths that are difficult to see from our everyday earth-bound perspective.

The buffalo represents a firm connection to the earth.

The bear represents the need for solitary reflection.

As a totem, mouse represents heightened awareness of little details and the importance of taking small, persistent action.

When you Shift consciousness and raise your vibrational frequency, you'll utilize all four spirit keepers of the Medicine Wheel.

> Eagle helps you see beyond your current situation.
> Buffalo keeps you grounded.
> Bear honors your time of inner reflection.
> Mouse helps you take small, persistent action as you move forward.

As your consciousness shifts, you'll notice new solutions to your current situation arising—ones you haven't thought of before. From this new vantage point, new insights and fresh opportunities will present themselves, and wisely chosen responses can be made. Then, you'll know what action or non-action to take. And you'll make better choices from an Eagle perspective.

Aim for the Highest Vibrational Experience

Three emotive states give you the highest vibrational experience. They are:

> Being love.
> Expressing gratitude and appreciation.
> Acts of forgiveness.

Being love is the most cherished emotive state. Love is one of the highest vibrational frequencies, and it has the power to heal and dissolve negative emotions.

Expressing gratitude and feeling appreciation feels good! As it's as if a thousand joyous, effervescent bubbles are flooding your system, mentally, physically, and emotionally.

When you practice acts of forgiveness, you're releasing the past. You're allowing the winds of change to blow away the suffering, sorrows, and burdens of the past to restore inner peace.

Being Love—How You'll Shift Consciousness

You can be love anytime, anywhere. Ram Dass reminds us. He shares his experience riding the bus in New York City:

> "In 1969, I was giving a series of lectures in New York City. Every night, taking the bus up Third Avenue, I got the same extraordinary bus driver.
>
> It was rush hour in one of the world's busiest cities, but he had a warm word and a caring presence for each person who got on the bus.
>
> He drove us as if he were sculling a boat down a river, flowing through the traffic rather than resisting it.
>
> Everyone who got on the bus was less likely to kick the dog that evening or be otherwise hostile and unloving because of the loving space the driver created. Yet all he was doing was driving the bus.
>
> He wasn't a therapist or a great spiritual teacher. He was simply being love.[1]"

One of the most extraordinary things about being love is that it can express itself in a variety of unconditional ways:

"Love is patient, love is kind. It does not envy, it does not boast, it is not proud. It does not dishonor others, it is not self-seeking, it is not easily angered, it keeps no record of wrongs. Love does not delight in evil but rejoices with the truth. It always protects, always trust, always hopes, always perseveres."[2]

Being love is the experience of moving from a contracted state to an expansive one. It's Shifting your energy from feeling stuck to feeling free.

How to Be Love

"Okay," I can hear you say, "That's all well and good. But how do you *exactly* do that?"

Good question!

Let's review what you know so far:

> **Step One**—You know how to See the situation and what you're experiencing for what it is.
>
> **Step Two**—You've learned how to Stop yourself from focusing on the mind stories by removing yourself from the drama. You've learned how to Be Still and breathe into the contracted places within your body.

Now that your mind is calm and your body is relaxed, you're ready to be love. Here's how:

Take a moment and think about someone you unconditionally love, someone you love without expectations, hopes, or desires. A newborn baby or a beloved grandmother are two possibilities.

When you think about someone you love, it could also be a special animal companion that fills your heart with joy. Family pets come to mind. Or even your horse; however, if you're finding this exercise a little bit challenging, that's okay. Most of us have complicated relationships with those we love. If that's true for you, then turn to nature for inspiration. A particularly stunning sunrise, a stand of flowering cherry blossom trees, or a placid lake reflecting the vibrant color palette of sunset.

In many ways, it doesn't matter who or what you focus your attention on; it's all about a feeling—the feeling of inward expansion.

My friend Namiko is a fan of forest bathing. "I love the sounds of the forest, the scent of the trees, and the way sunlight dances with them. Breathing in the fresh, clean air never fails to expand me, from the inside out."

But what about if you're stuck in your office. What do you do then?

My coaching buddy, Sun Jung, came up with a great solution. "I sit and focus on how much I love life. I know it sounds crazy, but my heart swells when I focus on loving life! After a while, the ups and downs don't matter, and I find myself in a wonderful place of expansion."

Forest bathing is Namiko's "go-to." Sun Jung goes on a rampage about loving life.

What about you?

Who or what expands your heart?

_____

_____

_____

_____

_____

_____

When it comes to Shifting your consciousness, it's been my experience that the emotive states of love and gratitude (more about that next) are the easiest to start with, even in situations where forgiveness is required.

Being love = expansion.

"And now these three remain faith, hope, and love. But the greatest of these is love."[3]

Feeling Gratitude and Appreciation—How You'll Climb the Vibrational Ladder

Have you read *The Book of Values* by Yael Eylat-Tanaka? This unique book explores 140 different values, inviting us to reflect and consider. Here's the one on gratitude:

> "I had a conversation with my son in which I asked him if he was happy. Without hesitation, he answered, "I'm extremely happy. I'm free to do what I want, when I want. My life is just good."
>
> I pondered that answer and felt some envy for his sense of freedom.
>
> I, by contrast, do not feel free. I feel weighed down by "stuff," responsibilities, my job, and limited finances. So, I put this question to a couple of friends: What is happiness? The answers came rapidly and authentically: Happiness is the state of accepting what one has with gratitude.
>
> Gratitude for the roses as well as their thorns. How profound. The difficulties in life are as precious as the successes and rewards. Without difficulties and strife, how would we

test our mettle? Where would we exercise judgment? How would we make choices?

I have, indeed, many things to be grateful for. Once I begin to focus on what I'm grateful for, from the most minuscule to the grand, I indeed feel happy, blessed, lucky, and proud of myself."[4]

Gratitude is powerful!

It's a heart-centered approach to being at peace with yourself and with all that you have.

As Eckhart Tolle says, "It is through gratitude for the present moment that the spiritual dimension of life opens up." And when you practice gratitude, you attract even more things to your life to be grateful for. This, then, raises your vibrational ladder.

How to Express Gratitude and Appreciation

Mother Teresa once said, "In this life, we cannot do great things. We can only do small things with great love."

I agree.

The word gratitude is derived from the Latin word *gratia* meaning grace, graciousness, or gratefulness. It's a thankful appreciation for what an individual receives, whether tangible or intangible. [5]

When you convey gratitude and appreciation, you're expressing the goodness in your life, and, as a result, connecting to something larger than yourself—whether it be other people, nature, or a higher power.

You can feel and express gratitude in any number of ways. After all, there's always something for which to be grateful. Here's how:

Take a moment, right now, and make a list of everyone and everything you feel grateful for and appreciate. Big or small, profound or straightforward, it doesn't matter.

To get your juices flowing, here are some of the people and things I'm grateful for and appreciate:

God, my spiritual mentors, angels, and ancestors who give me support and guidance along my journey.

My loving husband and my two wonderful boys.

My cousin Charis, who writes three things she's grateful for every day, and I do the same. Together, we keep the vibration high!

My job and the kind and caring people with whom I work.

How sunny and beautiful the mornings are when I walk to the pier to catch the ferry with my husband on the way to work.

For the times when I miss the bus and get to walk home looking out over the water and seeing a full moon.

For the times when my boys meet me off the ferry and walk me home after work.

For the times my family spends Sunday afternoons playing board games and have such great fun.

My sister, who's always very supportive of me.

My friends, who are understanding, encouraging, and bring joy to my life.

Now it's your turn. Crack open your journal and start your list on a new page or jot it down here.

_____

_____

_____

_____

_____

_____

_____

_____

_____

Don't you feel elated? Once you start, it's hard to stop. Isn't it?

This is why expressing gratitude and appreciation is so powerful. It makes you happy!

Just like with being love, it doesn't matter who or what you're feeling gratitude for and expressing appreciation for; it's all about a feeling—the feeling of happiness.

Being love + expressing gratitude and appreciation = happiness.

Practicing daily expressions of gratefulness and appreciation will exponentially raise your frequency vibration.

What Happens if I Don't Feel Grateful About Anything?

Yep. From time to time, that will happen.

It happens to me, too.

So, when it feels as if your world is crashing down around you, say "thank you." Or do as my mentor Debra Poneman does: take gratitude breaks throughout your day. She would look around her room and be thankful for everything she sees.

I would do the same by saying "thank you" for anything. I'd say "thank you" for my computer, for the stapler on my desk, and for the clean water that I was drinking.

When I can't find anything to be grateful for, I affirm that the universe is conspiring for my greatest good. No matter how dire it appears, my current situation has some kernel of wisdom within it for me.

Here's my thank you mantra when times are tough:

Thank you for this lesson.
The universe looks after me and is good to me. Thank you.
There's love in my life, and life is good to me. Thank you.

And just like that, your mind has been reconditioned to look at the positive side of things.

Keep saying "thank you" until you've worked your way up the vibrational ladder enough that you feel yourself expanding, and expressions of gratitude and appreciation flow easily from you. From there, it's a straight shot to being love.

Next thing you know, you're blessing everyone!

Inspirational Act of Forgiveness

On May 13, 1981, the unthinkable happened.

In front of thousands, in Rome's St. Peter's Square, Pope John Paul II, was shot. It was unimaginable that this happened to one of the most beloved and popular popes in the Catholic Church's history.

Four shots rang out, two seriously wounding the Pope and two more injuring people in the crowd. The Pope spent five hours in surgery and many more days recovering.

The man who shot Pope John Paul II was twenty-three years old. He was from Turkey and a member of a radical terrorist group.

As soon as Pope John Paul II was well enough, he visited his would-be assassin. On the way to the hospital, he decided to forgive the young man and publicly did so on May 17, 1981. Even after he left the hospital, Pope John Paul II frequently visited the imprisoned shooter.

What an inspirational act of forgiveness!

> Forgiving someone, whether yourself or another, means the drama is over. You're done with the pain and nightmare that keeps your mind spinning and your emotions churning. As American novelist Anne Lamott puts it in *Plan B:*

Forgiveness means it finally becomes unimportant that you hit back. You're done. It doesn't necessarily mean that you want to have lunch with the person. If you keep hitting back, you stay trapped in the nightmare.[6]

Forgiveness releases past hurts and ushers in peace.

"Not forgiving is like drinking rat poison and then waiting for the rat to die," declares Anne Lamott in *Traveling Mercies.*[7]

Being love + expressing gratitude and appreciation + forgiveness = peace.

Forgiveness, however, is more than paying lip service with an automatic, "I'm sorry."

The act of forgiveness I'm talking about is when you're able to let go—truly. Not because you should. But because you want to. You do it because peace is more important than holding on to hurt.

Truly letting go means Seeing the situation and what you're experiencing for what it is without labeling it as "good" or "bad."

The most powerful act of forgiveness is realizing that there really isn't anything to forgive. What upset you has passed. It's holding on to the problem that's still upsetting you and the judgments you're making about it.

No blame. No shame.

What happened is what happened.

Over. Finished. Done.

It's been my experience that even when you're facing a situation that you know would benefit from an act of forgiveness, it's much easier to start the Shift by expressing gratitude and appreciation.

"Thank you for the lessons I learned. I trust that everything happens for my highest good. Go in peace."

I alone cannot change society for the better. But I can radically transform my own consciousness, overturning the conditioning that limits my potential.
When you shift your consciousness, you shift your reality. ~ Anon.

CHAPTER 8

Your Emergency List

*Every time you're tempted to react in the same old way,
ask if you want to be a prisoner of the past or a pioneer of the
future. ~ Deepak Chopra*

When negative emotions run hot, it's nearly impossible to jump right
in and start being love or expressing gratitude and appreciation. And
forget about doing any acts of forgiveness!

This, I know.

I've tried the "fake it 'til you make it" approach of plastering a smile
on my face, saying, "I'm fine" when I'm not, and being the Queen of
Positivity when all I want to do is scream. My insincerity doesn't fool
anyone, and I feel beat up and bruised on the inside.

That's why having an Emergency List is so important.

It's my secret weapon. And it will be yours, too.

When to Use Your Emergency List

Whenever your emotional house is on fire!

So, if you walked into the living room and saw your curtains on fire,
what's the first thing you'd do?

Would you sit back and ponder the situation, wondering how it got
started? Or would you leap into action?

Leap into action, of course!

You'd sprint for the fire extinguisher, pull the pin, aim the nozzle, and squeeze the handle to release the extinguishing agent. Right?

Same with your Emergency List.

When your emotional house is on fire, negative emotions are running hot, and you don't want "to be a prisoner of the past," pull out your Emergency List and extinguish the flames.

This is the way you'll turn things around and Shift your energy into a higher vibrational frequency.

My Story

In the past, whenever I felt angry, upset, or even sad, I used to escalate it into a crisis and reach out to my husband to make it better.

Without regard to my husband or what he might be doing at work, I'd call him. In the middle of the day!

I can't believe I used to do that.

And what could he do, anyway?

He couldn't come rushing over to my office and make it all better. Heck, he couldn't even come to the phone most of the time. After all, he had his work to do. Besides that, if I called him to vent about my day and what had just happened, it would only upset him.

Talk about unrealistic expectations!

So, I figured out how to stop depending on others to fix my problems. My Emergency List is the way I help myself out of my red-hot emotional mess.

Very empowering, that was!

The Emergency List

Think of your Emergency List as your personal fire extinguisher and any negative feelings you're having as the smoke before the fire.

When you're tempted to react the same old way, use your Emergency List. When you feel yourself spiraling downward into a quagmire of negativity, pull out your fire extinguisher. When you want relief, your Emergency List is here for you.

The point of the Emergency List is to help you Stop yourself from focusing on the mind stories and the untruths it's spinning.

It's a list of things that will immediately help you feel better. It's your emotional fire extinguisher that you can pull out at any time.

It doesn't matter what's on the list. What's important is that whatever is on the list helps you Stop yourself from focusing on the spinning mind stories so you can focus on the present.

I always keep my Emergency List accessible. At. All. Times!

My Emergency List used to be on my computer screen and saved as an image on my smartphone. I even had a printed copy that I kept tucked in my wallet when pulling out my phone would be too conspicuous in a meeting. Now, my Emergency List is in my head.

And it's the gateway to Step One—See—that funnels me through The Formula.

My husband calls it my sanity saver. I call it my pain killer because it kills the pain inside enough so that I can lift off the burning emotions and start up the vibrational ladder.

It's how I pick myself up when "bad" things happen.

We all need an Emergency List.

Here's mine.

My Emergency List

1. Do Dr. Sue Morter's *Central Channel Breathing*. (I've placed a link to a YouTube video in the Notes section of this book, and describe how to do it in chapter 20).

2. Do Dr. David R. Hawkins's *The Mechanism of Letting Go*. (I talk more about this in chapter 23.)

3. Do Ho'oponopono—powerful Hawaiian prayer. (I talk more about this in chapter 18.)

4. See the whole, and realize that what I'm Seeing is only one piece of the puzzle. Trust that it's okay. Accept what is. Let go of resistance.

5. Ask myself, "How does it get better than this?" (I talk more about this in chapter 23.)

6. Focus on gratitude. Thank God or the universe for the situation and what I'm experiencing. I thank the "actor" who's teaching me the lesson.

7. Remind myself that all is well and that everything is happening for my highest good.

8. Focus on one second at a time. (I talk more about this in chapter 23.)

9. Call on my angels or God to help me get to a place of peace, or surrender the problem to the higher power.

10. Allow myself to feel good. Then I start Shifting consciousness and moving to a higher vibrational frequency by thinking about all the positive things in my life.

The minute I pull out my Emergency List and start working through it, I feel better.

The pain subsides, I'm out of my emotional black hole, and I can now reflect on what happened.

It feels good to move up the ladder!

Now it's your turn.

Your Emergency List

The most important thing about your Emergency List is that whatever you include must give you immediate relief. That means you can put anything you want on your Emergency List—as long as it helps you get out of your head, switch gears, and calm your emotions.

I have ten items on my Emergency List; however, there's nothing special about the number ten.

I suggest having at least five items, so you can pick and choose what to use in specific situations. And I caution against having too many because numerous possibilities will engage your mind causing it to become fixated on choosing the "right" one from the list. Then you'll become frustrated and overwhelmed.

It's best to stick to a group of easy-to-recall "go-to" items that you can automatically reach for when you need an emotional fire extinguisher.

Make it Meaningful

Many people have found that having a specific prayer or chant on their list works best for them. Lots of people like the Serenity Prayer written:

> "God, grant me the serenity to accept the things I cannot change,
> Courage to change the things I can,
> And the wisdom to know the difference.[1]"

Others find Psalm 23 from the Bible comforting and reassuring in times of strife:

> "The Lord is my shepherd; I shall not want.

He makes me lie down in green pastures.

He leads me beside still waters.

He restoreth my soul.

He leads me in the paths of righteousness for His name's sake.

Even though I walk through the valley of the shadow of death, I will fear no evil, for you are with me; your rod and your staff they comfort me.

You prepare a table before me in the presence of mine enemies; thou anoint my head with oil; my cup overflows.

Surely goodness and mercy shall follow me all the days of my life, and I shall dwell in the house of the Lord forever.[2]"

Personalize and Customize

Your Emergency List is yours. So, customize it any way you want. You can even include an image on your Emergency List if it helps you Stop focusing on the mind stories and Be Still and surrender. Images are potent conveyors of emotion, and the right one will quickly transport you to a relaxing, peaceful place.

Another way to personalize your Emergency List is by including a visualization to help relax you into a peaceful state.

Whatever works for you is what's right for you.

Keep your Emergency List with you—In your mind, in your space, and in your heart.

Train yourself to go to your Emergency List whenever you need to stop your mind from churning out stories that add to you feeling bad about yourself.

Now it's your turn.

Ready. Set. Go!

1. _____

2. _____

3. _____

4. _____

5. _____

6. _____

7. _____

8. _____

9. _____

10. _____

*Anytime you feel good, you've found vibrational alignment with
who you are ~ Abraham-Hicks*

PART II

Stop Chasing

CHAPTER 9

Approval

Approval is a lover who will always break your heart.
~ Sammy Rhodes

As human beings, we live in our heads. Sometimes it's the hopes and dreams of a perfect world where everything is precisely how we want it to be. Other times, it's the reliving of past hurts and disappointments.

Part II of *Start Chasing Nothing* is about learning how to be present and grounded in reality. Not a false reality of the mind but the current reality of the body. Instead of looking behind you or ahead of you, we'll look at how you can be fully conscious in the moment and free from the noise inside your mind.

It's not to say that your mind will stop yo-yo-ing between the past and the future. Rather, that it will do it less often, and you'll be less bothered by the stories your mind makes up.

To do that, we'll be redefining common areas that keep us stuck in the past, that prevent us from living in the present. Free from attachment to a specific outcome. Free from expectations of events or people. Free from guilt.

Together, we'll explore new ways of seeing, new ways of acting, and new ways of being.

Let's get started.

That quotation from minister, Sammy Rhodes is accurate. Seeking approval will always break your heart.

Those you're seeking approval from are fickle. Their standards change. Their expectations get amended. What they like and approve of one time may not be the same at another time.

Yet, chasing approval from others to validate ourselves is something we all do—some more than others. We chase approval as children. We crave validation as teens. We pretend we don't need anyone's approval as adults, and silently wither inside when we don't get it.

There's an evolutionary reason why we seek approval from others. And there's help for those who want to break free from the need to chase approval.

Our Need to Connect

Hardwired into all human beings is a need to connect with others. It's the primary driver behind our need for approval.

One of the foremost authorities in the field of social neuroscience is Dr. Matthew D. Lieberman. He and his colleagues have spent decades researching social connections. They've discovered that our need to connect is as fundamental as our need for food and water.

In an interview with *Scientific American,* Dr. Lieberman explains why social pain—rejection—feels as real as physical pain.

> "The things that cause us to feel pain are the things that are evolutionarily recognized as threats to our survival. The existence of social pain is a sign that evolution has treated social connection like a necessity, not a luxury. It also alters our motivational landscape.
>
> Across many studies of mammals, from the smallest rodents to us humans, the data suggests that our social environment profoundly shapes us and that we suffer greatly when our social bonds are threatened or severed.[1]"

Connection with others makes us feel loved and accepted. Rejection by others triggers fear. This is why disapproval stings so much.

Seeking Approval

Seeking approval for things you've done from authority figures in your life starts at a very young age. Parents clap when their child eats peas, teachers give stickers and gold stars when children excel, and piano teachers praise when a scale is properly executed.

As you get older, parents stop clapping when you eat a new vegetable, teachers give out grades instead of stars, and you have to play more challenging pieces if you want your piano teacher's praise.

By the time you're a teen, you already know to say "yes" when you want to say "no." You change your point of view, depending on who you're with, and wear clothes you don't really like, all to fit in.

You've felt the sting of rejection. You like feeling loved and accepted better.

By the time you're a young adult, chances are you're a stifled version of yourself. You've become a master at telling people what they want to hear so they'll approve of you, have difficulty expressing a different point of view, and would rather keep quiet than work through conflict.

There's such a thing as caring too much about another person's approval. And I say this as a self-confessed, approval-seeking, people-pleaser.

Try saying that five times fast!

My Story

Seeking approval is not a new chase for me.

As you know, I sought approval from my parents and teachers as a child, my peers as a youth, and my colleagues and bosses as an adult.

While I thought I had worked through much of my chase for approval, there was still a pocket of shame that needed healing.

> Many years ago, in a previous job, I had a boss I admired and I placed a lot of meaning on his approval.
>
> I chased his approval by getting to the office early, working hard throughout the day, and being one of the last to leave at night.
>
> My commute to and from work was an hour, so that meant I left home at 7:30 A.M., arriving thirty minutes before the workday started, and returned around 8:00 P.M. Yep. It was a long day of chasing.
>
> My home time is precious to me—I love being with my family. And spending quality time with my boys is my favorite thing to do; however, during the workweek, with me getting home so late, I only had two hours to spend with them before bed.
>
> Therefore, when I get to leave work early, I'm thrilled!
>
> One time, I left work at exactly 6:39 P.M. I got home an hour later, ate dinner with my family, spent time with my boys, and went to bed.
>
> When I arrived at work the following day, I saw that my boss had left a message on my office phone at 6:42 P.M.—*three minutes* after I left the previous day. My heart sank. I felt so badly about missing his call that I literally felt pain in my chest. Seriously. I'm not exaggerating!
>
> Within seconds, all the good feelings I carried with me from spending time with my family the night before were

gone. Poof. My peace of mind was shattered. My focus fragmented. I had traded peace for pain—all because I'd missed my boss's call.

And that's not all. Throughout the entire day, I felt horrible. My mood was depressed, my stomach hurt, and I couldn't stop admonishing myself for leaving work earlier than usual.

I should have stayed! Had I made a big mistake by leaving a little early? Had I failed dreadfully by not being there for his call? Did he think I was a bad employee?

Compounding this, a memory of me as a youth flared up, adding fuel to my already burning emotional pile.

I remembered a time in school when I'd done poorly on an exam. I was ashamed of my performance and eager to show my teacher that I could do better. But I had to wait two months before I could redeem myself. And all that time, I was sure my teacher was disappointed with me because I'd let her down.

That memory was the pocket of shame that needed healing. Was the teacher disappointed with me? Did she feel like I'd let her down? I don't know. The heartsick, stomach-sinking sensation, however, was the same.

All the while, my resentment grew.

What was I supposed to do, wait in my office for his call? Relinquish more of my precious home time? Ask my family to eat without me?

I can't control when my boss decides to call me.

Now I know that the answer is "no"; however, while I was being hijacked by a pocket of shame from the past, feelings of failure, not being enough, and disapproval crashed down upon me.

> Of course, I wanted to please my boss and do a good job
> for him. But at what cost? Chinese philosopher Laozi had
> it right when he said, "Care about what other people think,
> and you will always be their prisoner."

This is what happens when you chase after approval. You lose yourself.

Want Versus Need

If you're like me, then you'd like to have the approval of others, especially of those whose judgment you respect. Of course, you want their approval. But do you need it? Has your need for it crossed the line into chasing after approval for external validation of your intrinsic worth?

It's a fine line between want and need.

I want to be loved versus I need you to love me.

I want my boss to like what I do versus I need for him or her to approve of me.

See the difference?

I want something.

I need someone to do something so that I can feel love and approval. That's the line.

I like how American industrialist Andrew Carnegie puts it: "Do not look for approval, except for the consciousness of doing your best." He's talking about the external validation of what you already know—the *consciousness* of knowing that you did your best.

In other words, as Wayne Dyer says, "Enjoy everything that happens in your life, but never make your happiness or success dependent on an attachment to any person, place, or thing."

Want versus need. Energetically, you feel the difference. One feels comfortable, the other feels tight. One is allowing, the other needy.

It's an "and" not an "or."

You'd prefer to have the approval of someone *and* feel okay about it if you don't get it, versus you need the approval of someone *or* you won't feel worthy.

When you make your value reliant on what others think of you, you can't help but chase after approval.

It's About Self-Worth

*What the superior man seeks is in himself; what the small man
seeks is in others. ~ Confucius*

The more you chase approval from the outside, the less happy you'll feel on the inside. The smaller your self-worth, the greater emphasis you'll place on other-worth.

Merriam-Webster defines self-worth as "a sense of one's own value as a human being."[2]

Your self-worth comes from within, not from other people or other things outside of you. You are a worthy person, with or without the approval of others. You are the determiner of your actions. You don't need to be driven by the demand for approval.

Trust me. I know. I've spent most of my life seeking approval. The desire to get people to like and approve of me motivated most of my choices and actions in life—until it didn't.

The price you pay when you want someone's approval is pain. Pain obliterates peace. Obliterated peace disrupts pleasure and compounds pain. Author, Janet Attwood, calls this layering pain on pain. And the more you do it, the more pain-filled your life becomes.

When you want someone's approval, there's no denying the cost is high. In exchange for peace, you get pain—until you don't.

Yet, I'm here to tell you that all is not lost. Even if you're someone like me who constantly chased the approval of others, you, too, can get off that hamster wheel and break free.

Self-Approval Versus Other-Approval

The root cause of chasing for approval depends on someone or something outside yourself to validate who you are, endorse what you're doing or approve of what you've done. That's called other-approval.

The opposite of that is self-approval.

To approve of yourself, as you are right now, even if you're in the process of changing something about yourself. (And it's essential not to delay approving of yourself until then.) To appreciate who you are and what you have to offer.

Self-approval means that you're the source of your approval—not something or someone else. So instead of relying on others to approve, do it for yourself. Otherwise, you'll end up finding faults in yourself, whether someone else does or not.

Author, Louise Hay, is one of my favorite authors. She has this to say about self-approval:

> Remember, you have been criticizing yourself for years, and it hasn't worked. Try approving of yourself and see what happens.

You'll quickly realize that self-approval is nurturing and nourishing. It strengthens self-worth, improves your self-esteem, and promotes self-growth.

My Story—Do-Over

If I'd known then what I know now, I'd do things differently.

Isn't that true of everybody?

It was the fall of 2018, and I had just begun working with the three steps that would eventually become The Formula. Little did I know, at the time, that these three steps, along with the Emergency List, would change my life.

If I could go back to the morning I walked into my office at work and heard the message from my boss at 6:42 P.M., the first thing I would have done was pull out my Emergency List.

I'd start by doing Dr. Sue Morter's Central Channel Breathing to ground myself. Then, focus on one second at a time to restore my sanity. Once calm, I'd begin working through the steps.

Step One—See the situation for what it is.

It was a phone message. From my boss. Outside of regular work hours. It triggered a memory from my youth that needed to be healed. That's all. No drama.

Step Two—Stop and Be Still.

No need to try to figure things out. No need to solve any problem. No looking for solutions or trying to guess about anything. I'd let go and surrender to what I was feeling.

Knowing what the mind does—chews over the past and projects into the future. And knowing where my body resides—in the present, I'd drop into my body and breathe. This would stop me from engaging with past stories or future worries.

I'd sense where the contracted areas of energy were and release them by breathing into them. All the while saying, "I'm okay. Everything is okay. Thank you. All is well."

Step Three—Shift.

Now that I'm calm and centered, it would be time to climb up the vibrational ladder to a place of higher frequency vibration. Here, I'd have access to thoughts and actions that were aligned with my well-being and tethered to my inner knowing.

I'd feel my "cork bobbing," as Abraham-Hicks is fond of saying, and realize that all that happened was a gift. I would express gratitude for that gift and thanks for the healing.

From Emergency List to cork bobbing—fifteen minutes. Tops! That's all the time it would have taken to go from freaking out to being calm and centered. This is why having an Emergency List is so helpful!

The rest of my day would be great. I'd be focused, my mood would be light, and I'd smile instead of duck when I saw my boss.

What I know now that I didn't know then was who caused my pain. It wasn't my boss. It was me. It was me chasing after approval that caused the pain.

Let it Go

In words made famous by Elsa in Disney's 2013 animated film *Frozen*—"Let it go!"

Dear reader, you are enough. You don't need anyone's love or approval to feel that way.

What you think you need will never be found in another person; however, you can always find it within you. Look within and recognize that you are complete. You always have been. You are now. You don't need to chase anyone or anything to feel that way.

Let go of the need for approval and start focusing on loving yourself for who you are, not for who you think you should be so that you'll gain approval.

Honor who you are. Live your life from a place of integrity and authenticity.

"Needing approval is like saying your view of me is more important than my own opinion of myself," said Dr. Wayne Dyer.

What you seek is within. Valuing yourself is way more substantive than validation from others.

It's Your Turn

Take a moment and think about some of the things you do and how you seek approval.

Are you a people-pleaser at home and at work? Perhaps you're someone who volunteers for every committee at church or agrees to do what no one else wants to do in order to win someone's approval. There's no right or wrong answer.

Either pull out your journal and turn to a blank page or write down your thoughts here:

_____

_____

_____

_____

_____

_____

_____

_____

_____

Next, reflect on the people in your life from whom you chase approval the most. Who are they, and what do you want from them? Do you want love? Validation? Acknowledgment? To be seen and heard?

List who, and write about the what here:

_____

_____

_____

_____

_____

_____

_____

_____

_____

The final quotation at the bottom of this chapter is from author, Richelle E. Goodrich. She slams the lid on chasing approval from others by giving herself permission to move forward. "What do you mean I have to wait for someone's approval? *I'm* someone. *I* approve."

What three things do you now give yourself the approval to be, feel, or do?

1. _____

2. _____

3. _____

It's quite natural for strong emotions to emerge at this point. That's fine. Just let them come up. Don't push them down or aside. Instead, pull out your Emergency List and choose which items you need to get relief.

In this situation, which items worked best?

_____

_____

_____

Release and let go.

> *Don't be a football of other people's opinions. Don't worry about what others think about you. In fact, nobody has time to think about you. ~ Sri Sri Ravi Shankar*

CHAPTER 10

Control of Others

It isn't the mountain ahead that wears you out; it's the grain of sand in your shoe. ~ Anon

How true!

While the earliest instances of this quotation can be traced back to an anonymous source in 1916, it's world heavyweight boxing champion Muhammad Ali who made it famous.

Regarded as one of the greatest professional boxers of all time, Ali was the symbol of resilience and perseverance in the 1970s, returning to recapture the heavyweight title for the third time when he was thirty-six years old.

"The grain of sand in your shoe" refers to the everyday distractions that sidetrack and divert us from our journey. We see the mountain ahead of us, yet give our attention to the grain of sand in our shoe.

From slight irritation to golf-sized blisters, if you've ever been walking and get some sand in your shoe or a pebble stuck in the sole, you know what I'm talking about. That pesky grain of sand will drive you crazy.

Start Chasing Nothing means keep your eyes fixed on the big picture. Don't let the little things take you off course.

A New Look at That Grain of Sand

You don't need to have a dramatic wake-up call to make changes in your present-day life. In fact, it's better if you don't, as counterintuitive as that may sound!

Wake-up calls can nudge you awake at any time. They can be traumatic, such as an accident, illness, or loss of a loved one. Or, they can be bothersome, like a grain of sand in your shoe.

Like when I asked my youngest son to do the laundry, and he countered, "I'll do it after I finish playing my computer game." Grrr!

Little frustrations, slight irritations, and minor interpersonal frictions can lead to big fights. Don't let that happen.

Pay attention to the grains of sand. See them as something that will help you reach new levels of self-awareness and growth. See them as nudges that will help you awaken to who you are.

Good things, those nudges.

North Wind and the Sun

When I was a little girl, I fell in love with *Aesop's Fables.* One of my favorites was "The North Wind and the Sun."

> "The North Wind and the Sun quarreled about which of them was the stronger. While they were disputing with much heat and bluster, a Traveler passed along the road wrapped in a cloak.
>
> "Let us agree," said the Sun, "that he is the stronger who can strip that Traveler of his cloak."
>
> "Very well," growled the North Wind, and at once sent a cold, howling blast against the Traveler.
>
> With the first gust of wind the ends of the cloak whipped about the Traveler's body. But he immediately wrapped it closely around him, and the harder the Wind blew, the tighter he held it to him. The North Wind tore angrily at the cloak, but all his efforts were in vain.

Then the Sun began to shine. At first, his beams were gentle, and in the pleasant warmth after the bitter cold of the North Wind, the Traveler unfastened his cloak and let it hang loosely from his shoulders. The Sun's rays grew warmer and warmer. The man took off his cap and mopped his brow. At last, he became so heated that he pulled off his cloak, and, to escape the blazing sunshine, threw himself down in the welcome shade of a tree by the roadside.

Moral of the story—gentleness and kind persuasion win where force and bluster fail.[1]"

A New Look at Parental Control

Control is paradoxical—the more you exert, the less you have.

If you're a parent, you know *exactly* what I mean.

Some mothers take pride in imposing themselves into all aspects of their children's lives. Called "tiger moms," they unequivocally think they know what's best for their children and expect to be respected and obeyed by them.

Yikes!

That's a heavy burden for mothers to bear and children to endure. Is it any wonder that children of controlling parents rebel?

Here's the rub: Parental control is an illusion—the more you exert, the less you have.

Huh?

If you're a parent, I can already hear your "yes, but..." push back.

Stay with me, dear reader.

Children aren't slabs of clay for us to shape and mold into our expectations. They're complex beings with their own needs and wants. They think autonomously from us, experience emotions independently of us, and vehemently rebel against control.

Children innately know an awful lot about themselves. And they don't need us to "tiger mom" them. What they do need from us are love, trust, and guidance.

Therefore, no matter how right you think you are, trying to control what your children do or how they turn out is folly. Even if you can control them today, they'll inevitably rebel tomorrow.

"A bird cannot love freely when caged," reminds author, Matshona Dhliwayo. "You have to love with an open hand," adds motivational speaker, Brandon Bays.

Love and trust.

Control Is an Illusion

Ingrained within us is the belief that we're supposed to be in control of ourselves and our lives. To do that, not only must we control what *we* say and do, we also must control what *other* people say and do.

That's a massive amount of control—I'm tired just thinking about it.

There's an old Yiddish proverb, "We plan; God laughs."

So true!

The illusion of control is the belief that you can influence outcomes that are, in fact, beyond your ability to control.

When you expect, compel, or require others to do what you want them to do, you're imposing your will and dominance upon them. You're telling them you know best.

Is that arrogance, or what?

And if things don't go according to your "tiger mom knows best" plans and expectations, you get upset, complain, and throw in a guilt trip for good measure.

In short, you inflict a lot of pain and expend a lot of energy while trying to get others to do what you want them to do—especially those you love.

Ken Poirot, author of *Mentor Me,* reminds us that "Control and manipulation are not love; the outcome is a life of imprisonment, ultimately leading to deep-rooted feelings of resentment."[2]

So, what do we do?

My Story

One of the hallmarks of living in the moment, in the present reality, is letting go.

> My youngest son is a strong-willed boy—I admire that about him. He's a teenager with a fully developed sense of self and how he likes things to be. Sometimes, that conflicts with my expectations.
>
> Most nights, when I come home after work, I'm eager to sit down with him over a nice dinner and talk about his day. I pepper him with lots of enthusiastic questions and am hurt when he responds with a monosyllabic "fine" or "okay." One-sided conversations are tiresome!
>
> Most days, I keep my mouth shut and put up with it.
>
> Last night, I did not.
>
> I blew up!
>
> "I rushed home to have dinner with you after a long day at work, and all I get is 'fine?' How can you be so inconsiderate and disrespectful? You don't listen to me. You don't respect me. I'm your *mom!*"

I yelled.

He glared.

It wasn't pretty.

Later, after working through the steps of The Formula, I was able to See the situation and what I was experiencing more clearly—I wanted him to behave in a certain way so I could feel loved and respected.

I placed 100% of the responsibility for how I was feeling on my teenager. And when I felt rebuffed by his one-word answers and lack of engagement, I acted out my hurt by making him feel guilty.

Who was the child, in this case, I wonder?

What's the point of guilting someone into saying or doing something? Even if he had complied to keep the peace, it wouldn't have made me feel truly loved or happy.

Listen up, dear readers—nothing anyone does against their own volition will ever make you happy. At least, not in the long run.

Thankfully, there is another way.

Law of Detachment

I know you've heard of the Law of Abundance. But have you heard of the Law of Detachment? Well, it's a good one to know about when letting go of control.

In *The Seven Spiritual Laws of Success,* Deepak Chopra explains:

> "The ego believes that if it knows what is going to happen, then it has control.
>
> It likes to feel in control because it then believes it will feel safe and powerful. But in fact, the ego cannot be certain what is going to happen. It can only project forward based upon past conditioning. The wisdom of uncertainty lies in

the recognition that the ego really can't know the future. Furthermore, the compulsion to know what is going to happen based upon the past effectively limits your ability to create the most appropriate present out of the field of all possibilities.

Not having a certainty and agenda for how things must turn out allows you to develop a genuine sense of ease and security based upon your connection to the universe.

It frees you up to appreciate and feel grateful for what is around you right now, instead of trying to make it something else. And it makes life more interesting and fun when you allow yourself to participate in the ever-unfolding wonder of creation.³"

I know it sounds paradoxical when I say that you need to let go of control to be in control; however, if you can wrap your mind around this notion, you'll realize its truth.

The egoic mind freaks out when it considers letting go of control. Yet, it's only by letting go that gratitude and appreciation can enter. And with that comes new insights, possibilities, and options.

When you first start practicing detachment, you'll notice how free you feel, free to be you and free to accept others as they are.

The second thing you'll experience is deep, profound relief. Relief that you're no longer basing your happiness on what someone else says, does, or how a situation turns out.

Not your beloved husband, wife, partner, or family. Not your boss, best friend, or esteemed teacher. Not a longed-for promotion, new Kate Spade purse, or Club Med vacation. You, and you alone are responsible for your happiness. Nothing and no one else is, was, or ever will be the source of how you feel.

Which feels better to you? That *you're* in control of your happiness, or *someone else* is in control of your happiness?

Now you can see why the Law of Detachment is so beneficial!

Attach, and you give away your control to other people and things. Detach, and you're in control of you—of yourself, your responses, and your actions.

Attach, and your happiness is limited to what someone else says or does. Detach, and your happiness is "based upon your connection to the universe."

Said plainly, only you can make you happy.

Letting Go Starts with You

I bet you've heard the saying, "When you point one finger, three fingers are pointing back at you." Well, in the Navajo culture, if you point an accusatory finger at someone, it's a court of law offense. You'll go before a tribal elder and be criticized for pointing a finger at someone without first considering the three fingers pointing back at you.

Jesus said something similar in the Sermon on the Mount: "Why do you see the speck that is in your brother's eye but do not notice the log in your own eye."[4]

Letting go starts with you.

Merriam-Webster defines accepting as "Able or willing to accept something or someone."[5]

When you accept, you're indicating a willingness to acknowledge someone for who they are. It doesn't mean that you agree. It means you freely accept someone as they are without the need to control or manipulate.

My Story—Do-Over

In the above example, I wanted my son to sit down to dinner and have a pleasant conversation with me. I wanted him to respond to my queries with complete sentences. I wanted him to share his day.

That's what I wanted.

What he wanted was to be left alone.

He didn't want to share his day. He just wanted to eat dinner in peace.

If letting go begins with me, then instead of shouting and pointing an accusatory finger at him, I'd See the situation and what I was experiencing for what it was. Then, I'd Stop focusing on the mind stories and Be Still and surrender to what I was feeling. From this place of calm, I'd look at the three fingers pointing back at me and:

1. Let go of attachment.
2. Accept how my son wanted to be at that moment.
3. Trust that he knows what's best for him.

I certainly wouldn't have accused him of disrespecting me. Or jump to the conclusion that I was in any way less loved because of his actions.

Instead of attacking him, I would have accepted him. I would've trusted him to know what was best for him and accepted his decision to be quiet at dinner.

Accept, yes.

Control, no.

Now It's Your Turn

Take a moment and think of someone you're trying to control. Someone who's nudging you to awaken. Who is it? Either pull out your journal and turn to a blank page or write that person's name here.

_____

Going with the Navajo "one finger, three fingers" concept, write down some of the things you're pointing out to that person, things you think need changing so you'll feel better.

_____

_____

_____

Next, look at the three fingers pointing back at you. See the situation and what you're experiencing. Stop yourself from focusing on the mind stories. Be Still and surrender to what you're feeling.

What do you need to let go of? From what do you need to detach?

_____

_____

_____

What's the number one thing you need to accept about this person?

_____

_____

_____

It's quite natural for strong emotions to emerge at this point. That's fine. Just let them come up. Don't push them down or aside. Instead, pull out your Emergency List and choose which items you need to get relief.

In this situation, which items worked best?

_____

_____

_____

Release and let go.

God grant me the serenity to accept the things I cannot change, courage to change the things I can, and the wisdom to know the difference.

CHAPTER 11

The Past

Holding on is believing that there's only a past; letting go is know-
ing that there's a future.

~ Daphne Rose Kingman

"Ah, yes. Letting go of the past," I see you rolling your eyes. "Easier said than done," you sigh.

What if I told you that is *it is* easier done than you think?

If you've ever found yourself stuck in the past, replaying past hurts, and holding on to grudges or betrayals, you're not alone.

One thing that connects us as humans is our ability to feel pain. There's a reason why we remember and process painful events differently than happy ones—more on that later.

What's important to know now is that you're not alone.

I don't know anyone who hasn't felt stuck in the past and unable to move on, no matter how hard they tried. We've all experienced emotional hurt. We've all acted out past pains in present moments.

I've held grudges and ruminated about past betrayals, too. And there've been times when the pain consumed me to the point where I couldn't function.

When emotional pain prevents you from healing from a situation or event, it's a sign you need to let go of the past so you can move on.

Here's how.

Stop Being Hijacked by the Past

"Resistance is futile," so say the Borg in *Star Trek: The Next Generation*.

Many know that scene where Captain Jean Luc Piccard of the *USS Enterprise* made Star Trek franchise history when he was assimilated by the Borg. With half his face covered by robotic implants, he faced the screen and informed Commander William Riker:

> "I am Locutus of Borg. Resistance is futile. Your life as it has been is over. From this time forward, you will service us."

As dramatic as that pronouncement was, it's not that much different from when past hurts and painful memories hijack you.

When past experiences take over the present, our daily lives suffer. Like Jean Luc, his present moment ceased to exist. And when you base present-day decisions on painful past events, the present ceases to exist for you, too.

Why Do We Get Stuck in the Past?

We all know that the past is, well, in the past. We also know it can't be changed. So, why do we continue to relive it?

That's a great question!

According to neuroscience, the brain handles negative and positive information differently. Negative experiences require more time to process. That's why we're better at remembering and recalling painful events.

Remember vinyl records? Those 45 RPM records with the sound carved in the spiral grooves. The ones you have to play using a needle on a turntable.

They're making quite a comeback; however, there's a problem—when you obsessively listen to the same song, deep grooves form. And this creates a twofold problem. You can't play the previous song on the album without the needle sliding into the entrenched groove. And the needle can't get out of the trench to play any other song in the album.

That's what happens in your brain when you replay the past. You get stuck in the groove and can't get out.

That's why the steps of The Formula are so effective—they help you get out of the groove.

Letting Go of Attachment

So, how do you let go of past hurts and move on?

You start by letting go of expectations.

Tony Robbins is a premier performance coach with a bigger-than-life personality. He exudes confidence and charisma, inspiring and motivating people to become their best selves. He's spent more than 40 years creating breakthroughs and transforming lives.

But that's not how it was for him when he was younger.

Tony had a troubled childhood. His mother was a drug addict and alcoholic. His parents divorced when he was seven. By seventeen, he worked as a janitor after school and as a furniture mover on the weekends, making money to support his mother and siblings.

He left for school in the morning, went to work, came home to a dysfunctional family, woke up in the morning, and did it all again.

Talk about someone stuck in a groove!

Then one day, he decided to get himself out of the rut. He saved every penny he could and attended a Jim Rohn seminar. It changed his life. "I made this big decision to spend a week's pay to go to this event. I sat there, and I was mesmerized."

As we've talked about in this book, you don't need something big to happen to heed a wake-up call. You just need to pay attention to the nudges that come your way and take action.

> *To release the past, you must focus on your present.* ~ Tony Robbins

Why It's Hard to Live in the Present

Everyone from new-age philosophers to modern psychologists tell us to put aside past regrets and worries about the future. Focus on the present.

They make it sound easy!

For some, it is.

All non-human species do it effortlessly. Consider the family dog. I don't know of any better example of a non-human species living in the present. Dogs are right there, in the present. Sure, they remember past events; however, that's not where they dwell. No matter what's happened in the past, they're present, in the moment, greeting you with a joyful bark and an affectionate nuzzle; however, because we're human, living in the present takes more effort.

According to Eyal Winter, Ph.D., writing for *Psychology Today:*

> "Human psychology is evolutionarily hardwired to live in the past and the future.
>
> Other species have instincts and reflexes to help with their survival, but human survival relies very much on learning and planning. You can't learn without living in the past, and you can't plan without living in the future.

The other reason why it's so hard for us to live in the present is that . . . our mind views time as a continuous and linear process. Because it is continuous, any millisecond before the present moment is already past, and any millisecond later is already a future.[1"]

Is it any wonder why so many people have difficulty living in the present?

My Story

We live in an apartment in Hong Kong with a big living room window overlooking a bus stop.

One of the things I enjoyed when stepping off the bus after work was looking up and seeing my youngest son sitting on the windowsill, enthusiastically welcoming me home with a hale wave and cheeky smile.

It's hard to believe that it was only a few years ago when he was thirteen.

Today, no one waves me home.

He's "too old" for that now.

I often cry when I think of how he used to greet me. I miss it and the way he used to be. But it doesn't keep me from hoping that someday, he'll be there again. So, I look up.

Talk about being stuck in the past!

Now, he's a teenager and too busy playing on his computer to do much more than grunt "hi" when I come home.

At first, when he stopped greeting me from the window, I expressed how much I missed seeing him, expecting him to change. When he didn't, I, a tiger mom, guilt-tripped him into feeling bad about it. I cajoled, nagged, and complained. The more he retreated and closed himself off, the angrier I became.

> "What's wrong with you? Why aren't you happy to see me? I work hard all day, and you can't even come out of your room and greet me!"

Just like that, I had turned a perfectly wonderful memory into a painful loss.

If only he'd change, I'd feel better.

Talk about not taking responsibility for my feelings!

Blame Is a Three-Armed Bandit

Have you ever heard the adage, "When we blame others, we victimize ourselves"?

Think about it. This is another one of those "one finger, three fingers" examples. Pointing a finger when you think someone has done you wrong means there are still three fingers pointing back at you. And those three fingers are:

> Shame
>
> Martyr
>
> Victim

Shame because deep down inside, you know that the pain you're feeling has nothing to do with the present. It's about unmet expectations from the past.

Martyr because you know that the present suffering you think you're experiencing is really a storehouse of memories.

Victim because the helplessness you're undergoing is from a grooved and rutted song track from the past.

Past. Past. Past.

A New Look at the Present

What does it mean to be in the present?

There are lots of ways to describe being present. Some express it as being fully conscious of the moment and free from the noise of internal dialogue. For others, it's associated with feelings of stillness and peace. For all, there's the sensation of heightened awareness and greater aliveness.

I know it sounds cliché, but the present truly is all there is.

I once heard spiritual teacher, Master John Douglas, say that the whole world is happening at this present moment. That statement profoundly impacted me. Imagine the entire world happening now!

The present is a suspended state of mind. Here the past ceases to exist, and the future has yet to happen. "Life is now. Realize deeply that the present moment is all you have," says Eckhart Tolle.

Instead of looking behind or ahead, be in the present moment. Be in the now. Here, you're fully present and engaged without emotionally reacting to or attaching to your thoughts.

So, how do you do that?

Become the Observer

Remember in chapter four when I talked about sitting in the movie theater's balcony and observing the movie?

That's the best way to stay present.

Become the observer.

Instead of getting caught up in the movie and acting out your drama, See the situation and what you're experiencing for what it is.

Stop yourself from focusing on the mind stories. Be Still and surrender to what you're feeling.

In other words, detach from your thoughts and actions. Observe what's going on.

Focus on Your Heart

The other thing you can do is focus your attention on your heart.

Since the body lives in the present—the mind resided in the past and future—if you focus on the heart-space inside your body, you'll remain present.

That's what I do.

Throughout the day, I focus my attention on my heart and stay present.

By becoming the observer and focusing on your heart-space, you'll be present, happy, and content, no matter the circumstances.

The present is where it's at, dear readers!

My Story—Do-Over

If only I had stayed in the present!

In the above example, I wanted the son of my memories. I wanted him to be how he used to be. I wanted him to wait for my return and welcome me home with a hale wave and cheeky smile. I wanted the son who lived in my past.

Yet, he was living in the present.

By living in the past, I caused both of us pain: my son, for not living up to my expectations, and me, for expecting him to be a past version of himself.

If letting go of the past begins with me, then instead of blaming him, I'd first See the situation for what it was. Next, I'd Stop focusing on the mind stories and Be Still. After accepting and surrendering to what I was feeling, I'd breathe into the contracted areas of my body and release. Then I'd have a look at the three fingers pointing back at me and:

1. Let go of the past.
2. Accept my son in the present.
3. Become the observer.

I was stuck in the past. My son was not.

Finally, I would have done what Dr. Wayne Dyer recommends: "When given a choice between being right and being kind, choose kind."

Kind, yes.

Guilt trip, no.

Now It's Your Turn

Where are you stuck in the past? Is there a particular hurt that you can't stop thinking about? Is there someone who betrayed you that you can't let go of, or a grudge you've been holding onto for quite some time?

Take a moment and think about something that happened in the past that's nudging you to awaken. Either pull out your journal and turn to a blank page or write down what happened.

_____

_____

_____

_____

_____

_____

Since letting go of the past begins with you, See the situation and experience for what it is. Stop focusing on the mind stories, then Be Still and surrender.

Now, look at the three fingers pointing back at you. What three things do you need to let go of to be present?

_____

_____

_____

Taking Dr. Wayne Dyer's recommendation to heart, what does the event that's kept you stuck in the past look like now through the lens of kindness?

_____

_____

_____

It's quite natural for strong emotions to emerge at this point. That's fine. Just let them come up. Don't push them down or aside. Instead, pull out your Emergency List and choose which items you need to get relief.

In this situation, which items worked best?

_____

_____

_____

Release and let go.

To be kind is more important than being right. Many times, what people need is not a brilliant mind that speaks but a special heart that listens. ~ F. Scott Fitzgerald

CHAPTER 12

Façades

Be yourself; everyone else is taken. ~ *Oscar Wilde*

When my boys were little, they loved dressing up for Halloween. As soon as October rolled around, they'd start talking about who they wanted to be and what they were going to wear. And, of course, no costume was complete without a mask. They loved trying them on and acting out different characters. It always amazed me how easily they'd transform themselves into gypsies, giant pumpkins, and the Tin Man from *The Wizard of Oz* just by donning some clothes and putting on makeup.

Isn't that the same for you, too?

Who hasn't dressed for success and applied makeup when going to a job interview? Or put on a happy face and said, "I'm fine" when they weren't.

Let's face it—we all put on façades.

The problem comes when we're not aware of wearing a façade, or that there are so many layers of masks that we don't know who we are without them.

How many masks have you worn in your lifetime?

I've worn a lot!

Growing up, I wore the obedient and respectful Asian child mask. Also, the smart, overachieving daughter mask. Then, I wore the successful career woman mask while wearing the perfect wife and tiger mom masks.

Here's the rub—if you'd asked me ten years ago if I knew I was wearing these and many other masks, I would have said, "No way. You're crazy!"

I was doing what was expected of me.

No big deal. Right?

Well . . .

The Façade Is an Illusion

Are you familiar with the *trompe l'oeil* style of painting?

I'm sure you've seen it.

Trompe l'oeil means "to deceive the eye." Artists use it to create the illusion of reality. And once you know what you're looking for, you'll see it in fine art paintings from ancient Greece to the present; however, it's not limited to fine art paintings. Theater and movie sets use *trompe l'oeil* to create the illusion of buildings, towns, and worlds. Even interior designers use it to fashion illusionary landscapes and architectural features.

The Copenhagen Zoo has a very convincing *trompe l'oeil* featuring a giant snake crushing a bus.

Trompe l'oeil is fun.

Dressing up for Halloween is fun.

Chasing a façade is not.

Chasing Façades

What do I mean by chasing façades?

I'm sure you've heard the phrase "Fake it till you make it." It's something others tell us to do in situations where we feel awkward, intimidated, or unsure how to proceed.

Take it from me—"Fake it till you make it" comes with a very high price!

Not only is faking it emotionally, mentally, and physically draining, it's exhausting pretending to be someone you're not.

And when does the pretending stop?

After you feel confident? After you feel happy? After you feel strong?

Not for me.

Pretending is another one of those hamster wheels that's difficult to get off.

Sadly, I've done a lot of faking it in my life.

I've faked courage at meetings when feeling insecure inside. I've affected tolerance when something someone did or said upset me. I've plastered a smile on my face and faked happiness when inside I was crumbling. I've even put on the mask of "all is well" when my world was crashing down around me.

The thing is, you can't really fool yourself.

In *The Confidence Code,* authors Katty Kay and Claire Shipman explain the cost of faking it:

> "Attempt this bit of pop psychology at your peril!
>
> When you feel as if you need to be someone or something other than who you really are, it is a huge drain on your mind and body. It's very draining to regularly act like you feel one way when you feel another.
>
> Not only does faking it not work as a confidence booster, but it also almost certainly makes us feel less secure because knowingly masquerading as something we're not makes us anxious.[1]"

All this energy spent on chasing a façade pollutes and dilutes the beauty of you.

Have courage and be your true self.

The Man in the Iron Mask

Remember the movie *The Man in the Iron Mask?* It's the 1998 Four Musketeers movie—"one for all and all for one"—starring Leonardo DiCaprio as Phillipe, the enigmatic man behind the iron mask.

After a daring rescue from the Bastille by fellow musketeers Aramis, Athos, Porthos, and D'Artagnan, the man behind the mask faces a pivotal decision: Remove the mask or keep it on.

> "I've worn this mask for so long; I don't feel safe without it."
> "We feared the mask would destroy you."
> "I wear the mask. It does not wear me."

I often reflect on the choice that Phillipe made. He could have stayed hidden behind the mask. Maybe it would have been safer for him to do so. Instead, he tapped into his inner strength and courageously chose to take off the mask.

Why We Live Behind Masks

Wearing a mask allows you to present what you believe to be a better, more acceptable version of your real self to others.

Psychologists call this the imposter syndrome—pattern of behavior where people doubt their accomplishments, and they have a persistent, internalized fear of being exposed as a fraud.

The three defining characteristics of someone with imposter syndrome are:

1. A sense of being a fraud.
2. Fear of being discovered.
3. Difficulty internalizing success.

Check.
Check.
Check.

My Story

Yep. That was me. And without The Formula, it still would be.

> I've felt like a fraud for most of my life and feared being "found out." I had difficulty accepting compliments and felt embarrassed when receiving them. Therefore, I brushed them off.
>> "Thanks, it's no big deal."
>> "I just got lucky."

As nonsensical as this may seem, it somehow felt *wrong* receiving praise and acknowledging congratulatory milestones. Sincerely replying, "Thank you. I worked hard for that, and am so happy about getting it," was difficult for me.

Instead of celebrating, I chased. I was always worried that others would discover the truth. So, back to the grindstone I'd go, studying for more degrees, striving for more advancements, and racking up more trophies—my hamster wheel life.

Yet, behind my façade of success, I suffered from chronic self-doubt. I denied my worth, undervalued my abilities, and dreaded failure. The fear that the world would find out who I really was—a fraud— kept me awake at night.

Is it any wonder I had difficulty getting out of bed in the morning?

So, I pretended to be strong, that I had it all together, and that everything was "fine"—my positive persona wrapped up in an ever-present fake smile.

Sadly, I masked the amazing woman I was with an elaborate *trompe l'oeil.*

What was the cost, you ask?

Authenticity.

A New Look at Authenticity

Merriam-Webster defines accepting as "Being true to one's own personality, spirit, or character."[2] I like that definition.

Being true means knowing who you are and accepting yourself as you are. It means being faithful to, and factual about the truth about you.

Fourteenth-century monk, John Lyndgate, said, "You can please some of the people all of the time, you can please all of the people some of the time, but you can't please all of the people all of the time"

To which I ask, "Why bother?"

Some people believe that the key to being liked and accepted is by trying to please others.

Yikes!

Listen up, dear reader—you can never please anyone. No matter how hard you try. Someone somewhere is going to have reasons for not liking what you say or what you do. And there's nothing you can do about that.

"Let it go," sang Elsa in Disney's *Frozen.*

"This above all: to thine own self be true," penned Shakespeare for Polonius in *Hamlet.*

Give up people-pleasing! Be true to yourself and stop worrying about pleasing other people or living by someone else's standards.

Here's your new mantra: I will do what I want to do and speak whatever I need to say at the appropriate time. Those around me will eventually adjust.

That's being authentic.

Authenticity is about living in the present with conviction and confidence and staying true to yourself.

As Don Miguel Ruiz says in his book, *The Four Agreements:*

> "Be impeccable with your word. Speak with integrity. Say only what you mean. Avoid using the word to speak against yourself or to gossip about others. Use the power of your word in the direction of truth and love.[3]"

Authenticity Is a Process

If the thought of speaking your truth and being your true self has you quaking in your boots, join the club.

At first, when you let go of the façades and take off the masks, you're going to feel exposed. Naked, even.

That's totally normal.

Brené Brown, Ph.D., is one of my favorite authors. She's a research professor who's dedicated her life to studying and understanding humanity. One of her specialties is vulnerability. And because of her findings, she's single-handedly transformed the stereotype attributed to vulnerability into a courageous act of power.

Here's what she says about being authentic:

> "To be authentic, we must cultivate the courage to be imperfect—and vulnerable. We have to believe that we are fundamentally worthy of love and acceptance, just as we are. I've learned that there is no better way to invite more

grace, gratitude, and joy into our lives than by mindfully practicing authenticity.[4]"

Remember, dear reader, becoming authentic is a process.

Letting Go of the Façade Begins with You

There will come a time in your life when you're sick and tired of all the masks you're juggling. When pretending becomes a burden, and the illusion feels hollow. That's when you'll know that it's time to let go of the façade.

Since you're reading this book, I suspect that time is now.

Letting go of the façade is a courageous choice.

We aren't born with masks. We put them on. That means "the mask does not wear you." You have the power to remove the mask.

Take off your mask.

Let go of the façade.

Show your beauty to the world.

Dr. Elizabeth Kubler Ross explains, "Our concern must be to live while we're alive—to release our inner selves from the spiritual death that comes with living behind a façade designed to conform to external definitions of who and what we are."

Gandhi encourages, "Be congruent. Be authentic. Be your true self."

Dr. Brené Brown emboldens, "Vulnerability is having the courage to show up and be seen when we have no control over the outcome. Vulnerability is not weakness; it's our greatest measure of courage."

Why You Must Let Go

It takes a lot of energy to maintain a façade!

Physically, it's hard on your cardiovascular system to don a different personality. Emotionally it's isolating because people in your life don't know who you *really* are. And mentally, it's exhausting.

When you hide too many parts of yourself behind an illusion, you begin thinking the *trompe l'oeil* is real, that how much money you make, how chic you look, and where you go on holiday defines your worth. And that the number of trophies sitting on your shelf and diplomas hanging on your wall determines your value.

It isn't. And they don't.

Without shedding the façade, "the mask will wear you."

You can do this!

The Grass Is Greener on the Other Side

I know. I know. Everyone has experience with the grass not being greener on the other side; however, this is one of those times when *it is!*

Once you start letting go of the façade and aligning what you say and do with who you are, remarkable things will happen.

First, you'll feel relief.

Second, now that you've released the energy spent maintaining a particular image, you won't have to "put on a show" anymore!

As you begin accepting yourself and other people for who you and they are, and not for how much money they make, how they look, or where they work, you'll start having more genuine experiences. You'll feel more at ease, and people will feel more comfortable around you because you've stopped judging them.

When your words and actions become congruent, you'll be able to express your emotions and articulate your thoughts more freely.

As you become more of your true self, you'll find it easier to be transparent and honest with others. You'll be more open-minded. You'll take personal responsibility for yourself without feeling the need to blame others.

Because you're creating more meaningful connections, superficiality melts away. Relationships deepen. Other like-minded people will come into your life.

Finally, when you let go of the façade and become your true self, you'll know, for sure, that you're loved for who you are and not for the mask you've worn.

Let go of the façade.

Forge a path to your true self.

You'll like and appreciate your true self.

Now It's Your Turn

Letting go of the façade begins with identifying the masks you're wearing. Remember, it's a process.

To begin, pull out your journal and turn to a blank page or pen your answers here. Start by Seeing the situation and experience for what it is. Stop yourself from focusing on the mind stories. Instead, Be Still and surrender to whatever you're feeling.

Now, ask yourself, "What's one of the masks I'm wearing?"

_____

Explore why you're wearing it.

_____

_____

_____

_____

_____

_____

Who's with you when you're wearing this mask?

_____

Ask yourself, "What did I *use to* think was the benefit of wearing this mask?"

_____

_____

_____

_____

_____

_____

"What do I *now know* to be the cost of wearing this mask?"

_____

_____

_____

_____

_____

_____

List three things that you'll benefit from when you remove this mask.

1. _____

2. _____

3. _____

How are you feeling?

_____

_____

_____

It's quite natural for strong emotions to emerge at this point. That's fine. Just let them come up. Don't push them down or aside. Instead, pull out your Emergency List and choose which items you need to get relief.

In this situation, which items worked best?

_____

_____

_____

Remember, "Weebles wobble, but they don't fall down." Same for you. Nonetheless, when you do wobble and catch yourself reaching for a façade, turn to The Formula and go through the steps.

Step One—See the situation and what you're experiencing for what it is.

Step Two—Stop yourself from focusing on the mind stories. Be Still and surrender to what you're feeling.

Step Three—Shift by climbing up the vibrational ladder to a place of higher frequency vibration. From this vantage point, new insights and fresh opportunities will present themselves, and wisely chosen responses can be made.

Release and let go.

Owning your story and loving yourselves through the process is the bravest thing that you will ever do. ~ Brené Brown.

CHAPTER 13

Success Models

Two roads diverged in a wood, and I—I took the one less traveled by, and that has made all the difference. ~ Robert Frost

It seems like everyone is obsessed with success these days. Yet, what exactly is success?

What does it mean to be successful?

If you're reading this book, I bet the traditional way your parents and grandparents thought about success isn't how you think about success, that the standards of success they accepted and adopted for themselves don't resonate with you anymore. Maybe they never did. And you're tired of the struggle.

If this is the case, you're not alone, dear reader.

Debra Poneman, founder of the Yes to Success program, has been my mentor since 2017. Debra's helped thousands of people find true success, and I credit her for "switching on the light" around my struggle with success. Debra helped me understand that the success model I had inherited was outdated.

Because of her, I now define success more harmoniously and happily. In *The 5 Secrets to a Life of True Success,* Debra has this to say about success:

> "So, we all know that the days of thinking that success is only about money, or fame, or a big house, or a nice car,

or even a bestselling book are over. There isn't one of us who doesn't know people who have all that and more, who smile on the outside and are dying on the inside. Slowly but surely, people everywhere are coming around and recognizing that success is not an outside job. The old success was about material possessions, titles and fame, accolades, and a corner office.

But the new success is something else entirely.[1"]

Tradition View of Success

Were you ever told that to be happy you needed to be successful?

Yep. Me, too.

Our parents and grandparents believed that if they worked hard, they'd succeed. And if they were successful, that meant that they'd "made it." And if that happened, then they'd be happy.

Ideas about what success is and what it means to succeed pass from generation to generation. No blame here. It's the way things are when society and culture intersect with family values.

According to Merriam-Webster, success is defined as "the attainment of wealth, favor, or eminence." [2] In other words, wealth, respect, and fame.

The problem with this is that when success is expressed as a prescribed result, there's no room for personal manifestation. Being successful then becomes all about conforming, meeting expectations, and attainment. As a result, we delay personal happiness until after the goal is achieved.

Yikes!

Does the Tradition Definition of Success Work?

Based on the overabundance of self-help books, entrepreneurial podcasts, and interviews with people who've "made it" by the traditional view of success, I'd have to say, "No."

The demand for insight into how entrepreneurs went from rags to riches is insatiable; however, it's all a waste of time. Neither the desire to be successful nor knowing how anyone else did it will make much of a difference in how things turn out for you.

Why?

Because just as there are no two snowflakes exactly alike, no two people are the same. Therefore, even if you copied what Oprah Winfrey, Walt Disney, Steve Jobs, Elon Musk, or even my mentor Debra Poneman did to become successful, it doesn't guarantee that you will be.

Take that in, dear reader—you won't be successful following in someone else's footsteps.

Success means different things to different people. It changes with you as you grow. While going to Aruba over spring break might have been important to you at one stage of your life, it's not later. Same with affluence, wealth, or acquiring things.

Society tells you that success means having money, marrying the right person, owning a big house, driving a fancy car.

I say success is understanding what makes you truly happy. In your heart. Following your heart's guidance when pursuing goals, knowing it will evolve and change through time.

Chasing Success

We've all chased success.

How do you know if you're chasing success?

You know when you find yourself rushing through life instead of savoring it. When you're never content for long with what you have. When all your energy is directed at chasing after a goal that's "better than," "greater than," or "richer than" what you currently have.

If you find yourself hurrying through your moments, thinking there's always something better, always something you need to achieve, you're chasing success. As if you have to be successful, or be someone to justify your existence.

Chasing success saps your energy and drains your soul.

Here's the thing, dear reader—if you chase it, achieving it will only bring you momentary happiness. And no matter how far you climb or how much you earn, there's no guarantee you'll be happy.

It's far more valuable to focus on what's right in front of you than trying to live up to some future goal expectation.

New Success

How we define success is changing.

In 2014, Strayer University ran a national survey of 2,011 Americans 18 years and older. Called the Success Project Survey, it asked one question: "What does success mean to you?"

Astonishingly, 90% of Americans believe that success is defined by happiness more than money, respect, and fame!

Dr. Michael Plater, president of Strayer University, has this to say about the results:

> "This indicates a clear change in the way Americans are thinking about their personal journey. It's no longer about the car or the house. Instead, people are focused on leading a fulfilling life.[3]"

Wow! Right?

People are pushing back against the imprinting they've inherited from their family, culture, and society. They're seeing and defining success differently.

New success is about heart success.

Out are the traditional status symbols of success.

Out is the need to prove anything to anyone.

In are healthy, balanced lifestyles.

In is following your dreams.

In is finding meaning and contentment in your life.

And here's how to do it:

> Follow your unique path, and no one else's.
>
> Go where your heart leads you.
>
> Draw on your intuition and inner wisdom.
>
> Follow your curiosity.
>
> Pay attention to how your body feels.
>
> Do things that make you happy.
>
> Be compassionate and giving.

Yeah!

That's how new success looks.

In Thrive, Arianna Huffington explains why redefining what it means to be successful is necessary:.:

> "Our relentless pursuit of the two traditional metrics of success—money and power—has led to an epidemic of burnout and stress-related illnesses and an erosion in the quality of our relationships, family life, and, ironically, our careers.[4]"

She adds, "There is far more to living a successful life than just earning a bigger salary and having a corner office."[5]

Debra Poneman asserts, "It's not, 'I'm crushing these sales,' it's, 'I'm changing lives with my great product, and I'm grateful so many people will get to experience it.'"

Oprah Winfrey affirms, "The key to realizing a dream is to focus not on success but on significance."

I like that.

Focus on significance.

Be the best person you can be.

My Story

As you know, I wrestle with inherited family standards and norms. And even though I've redefined how I think and feel about success, I still struggle with comparing myself to others and coming up short.

Most days, I feel quite good about my life and what I've accomplished. On other days, I do battle with the whack-a-mole voice inside my head that tells me, "Yeah, that's good. But not good enough."

Woulda. Coulda. Shoulda.

Nope.

I am not getting back on that hamster wheel!

After decades of chasing, wanting to have more success to feel successful, I've learned a powerful truth—success is a continuous process.

Success isn't a destination. It's not "the end." Success is a journey that changes over time.

Best yet, I learned that I didn't have to put off being happy until I reached my "success destination." I can be happy every day, in every moment, along the journey.

There's no one-size-fits-all blueprint of success to follow. There's nothing you need to attain or anyone you need to please so that you'll be successful.

Success is the ability to feel good about yourself in all you do, be, and have. It's to enjoy and be grateful for everything, even money.

I've learned that the key to success is to be present and focus on the moment. To express gratitude for what I have. To appreciate those around me. When I do that, I feel great!

Debra Poneman calls this self-mastery: once you master your thoughts and make choices based on what makes you feel happy, when you exercise your ability, in every moment, and to choose how you feel and what you do.

A New Look at Success

Recently, I heard an interview with actor George Clooney about success, how he defines it and how he achieves it. Here are some of the things he said:

> "It's important to follow through on the promises you make. If you have the means to give back to your community and help those who are less fortunate, it's good for the world. Remain humble. Be selective and confident in your choices. Allow your failures to motivate you. Be yourself. Resolve conflict as positively as you can. Listen to understand. Never give up.[6]"

George Clooney speaks of integrity.

Thirteenth-century mystic Rumi speaks of favor: "Live life as if everything is rigged in your favor."

Selected verses from Max Ehrmann's prose poem "Desiderata" speak of peace:

> "Go placidly amid the noise and haste and remember what peace there may be in silence. As far as possible, without surrender, be on good terms with all persons.
> Speak your truth quietly and clearly and listen to others.
> Enjoy your achievements as well as your plans. Keep interested in your own career, however, humble.
> Nurture strength of spirit to shield you in sudden misfortune. But do not distress yourself with dark imaginings.
> Be gentle with yourself. You are a child of the universe.
> And whether or not it is clear to you, no doubt the universe is unfolding as it should. Therefore, be at peace with God.
> And whatever your labors and aspirations, in the noisy confusion of life, keep peace with your soul.
> Be cheerful. Strive to be happy.[7]"

Integrity. Favor. Peace. Live your life, knowing that the universe is conspiring for your greatest good and unfolding as it should.

How's that for a new view of success?

Achieving New Success

"Okay. That's great," I hear you saying, "How, exactly, do I achieve this new success?"

I asked that same question of Debra Poneman when I signed up for her Yes to Success program. Here's what she had to say:

> "Creating a foundation of inner silence through regular spiritual practice is essential. Live life in an effortless flow

instead of struggling against the tide. Discover and live the path of your destiny. Engage in sacred activism and selfless service."

And in the words of her first spiritual teacher, Maharishi Mahesh Yogi, "When love comes, let it flow. Don't stop it with your thinking."

Just as there are no two snowflakes exactly alike, there's no one path to success. I developed The Formula to help you uncover what's important to you.

Now It's Your Turn

People everywhere are taking a closer look at their individual situations and priorities and creating new, personalized definitions of success.

Now it's your turn.

This is going to be fun!

Once again, pull out your journal and turn to a blank page or write your answers here. You'll begin by looking at the traditional success model that was imprinted on you. See it for what it was. Stop yourself from focusing on any mind stories that come up. Be Still and surrender to what you're feeling.

Now, ask yourself, "What are some of the ways I was conditioned to think about success? What did it mean to my family to be successful?"

_____

_____

_____

_____

_____

_____

How did that impact me?

_____

_____

_____

Is that old success model working for me now?

_____

Next, you get to define *your* success model. What does new success look like to you?

_____

_____

_____

_____

_____

_____

If you were going to create a new success definition for yourself, what would it be?

_____

_____

_____

List three things you're grateful for, going forward:

1. _____

2. _____

3. _____

How are you feeling?

_____

_____

_____

It's quite natural for strong emotions to emerge at this point. That's fine. Just let them come up. Don't push them down or aside. Instead, pull out your Emergency List and choose which items you need to get relief. In this situation, which items worked best?

_____

_____

_____

Release and let go.

We don't see the world as it is; we see the world as we are.

- Maharishi Mahesh Yogi

CHAPTER 14

Money

A happy life starts with happy money. ~ Ken Honda

Money comes, and money goes. Where it goes, I do not know!

Has this been your experience with money?

It's certainly been mine!

As strange as this is—the more money I earned, the more money I spent. And I had no idea where it all went! It's not like I went on spending sprees! Did I have a hole in my pocket?

Yes! I did have a hole. Just not in my pocket.

Our Love-Hate Relationship with Money

If you have a love-hate relationship with money, you're not alone. According to Kyle Cease, author of *The Illusion of Money*, "Your relationship to money is just a mirror of your relationship to yourself."[1]

We all have a unique relationship with money. Sometimes we have a good relationship; other times, a poor one.

To see where you are along the love-hate continuum, check in with these money-related questions. Keep track of how many times you say "yes." Do you:

1. Worry about not having enough money?
2. Feel guilty when you spend it?
3. Think you need to have a certain amount to be happy?

4. Blame circumstances or people for your money woes?

5. Resent people with money?

6. Pretend as if you don't care about money?

7. Spend money you don't have?

8. Frequently make excuses for why you don't have enough money?

9. Spend more than you earn?

If you answered "yes" to most of these questions, you could improve your relationship with money.

Yet, no matter where you fall along the love-hate continuum, you can have a great relationship with money.

But first, you have to stop chasing dollars.

Chasing Dollars

What do I mean by chasing dollars?

If you frantically run around desperate for more money and buy things to make yourself feel better—you're chasing dollars.

Worry and neediness drive this pursuit in your effort to feel "all right," but we have all been told that money can't buy happiness.

While it's true that money doesn't buy happiness, it can make you feel happy, at least for a little while. And sometimes that little bit of joy tricks you into thinking that if you only bought more things or made more money, you'd feel happier, longer.

But it never works out that way, and you end up chasing more. Cease explains: "When we're chasing something, we're not actually chasing the thing; we're chasing the experience and feeling that we think the thing will give us." [2]

Have you ever watched children opening their gifts at Christmas? They run to the pile and tear off the wrapping paper, eager to see what's inside. Then, after a few joyous moments, they're on to the next box. And the next. And then the next.

I'm sure you've experienced this for yourself.

You see something. Buy it. You're thrilled to have it. And then the feeling's gone, and you're onto something else.

That's called chasing the experience.

It's another hamster wheel!

Now, I'm not saying that money is bad or that it's "the root of all evil." Not at all. I love money!

Having money, however, won't stop you from chasing. You'll chase forever until you "keep your life free from love of money and be content with what you have."[3]

My Story

I've worked very hard and been blessed with some significant promotions throughout my career. As a result, I make a good living and can buy what I want; however, I've chased money most of my life, trying to fill the emptiness I felt. And I thought by having more money and buying more things that I'd fill that void.

That never happened.

On reflection, I realize that I chased money and bought things because I didn't feel I was enough. I wasn't enough as a daughter, enough as a mother, enough as a friend, or enough as a colleague.

The void I was trying to fill was the false belief of not enough.

You see, deep down inside, I didn't feel that I *was* enough. Therefore, I compensated by wanting more, spending more, and getting more. Then, I'd feel guilty about my spending and berated myself for not saving.

I worried about not having enough money, fretted about spending money, and was anxious about not saving money.

Around I'd go on my hamster wheel of money woes.

I hadn't yet learned how to tap into my internal abundance.

Worrying About Money

I hate worrying about money. And I know you do, too. Yet, worrying about money is such a part of today's culture that it's become ubiquitous.

Here's the thing, dear reader—worrying about money hurts more than it helps.

Worry causes stress.

Worrying impedes your ability to think clearly and make good decisions.

Worry puts a strain on all your relationships and can lead to everything from tension headaches and stomach ulcers to heart attacks and strokes.

At its core, worry is a negative affirmation of what you *don't* want. You want money, but you're fixated on the lack of it. That means you're affirming lack! And that escalates into fear.

If you're feeling fear around money, you know how hard it is to stop worrying about money. It's a vicious cycle!

"Okay, I get it. I need to stop worrying about money. Right?"

"Yes."

"What, then?"

"You need to kintsugi your money woes!"

The Art of Kintsugi

Have you ever heard of kintsugi? It is the Japanese art of repairing broken pottery by mending the broken fault lines with lacquer dusted with gold, silver, or platinum.

The origins of Kintsugi date back to the Muromachi period when Ashikaga Yoshimitsu was the shogun of Japan.

The story goes that when Yoshimitsu's favorite tea bowl broke, he sent it to China for restoration. When it came back, however, the pieces were joined together with metal staples, disfiguring the bowl.

Horrified, Yoshimitsu beseeched his craftsmen to figure out a way to make his tea bowl whole again. First, they removed the metal staples and laid out each of the broken pieces. Then, instead of disguising the damage, they turned the fault lines into beautiful gold seams.

In this way, Kintsugi transformed the shogun's broken tea bowl into a beautiful work of art.

The art of Kintsugi isn't just for broken pottery pieces.

Fix the Hole

When my children were little, they loved going to the beach and playing in the sand. Our family would go often, and they never tired of digging holes with their plastic shovels and then filling them with endless buckets of seawater.

One day it happened. A crack formed in their little red bucket, and it began leaking. And no matter how quickly they ran from the ocean to the hole they were digging, they never could keep enough water in their bucket to fill the hole.

That's the same when chasing money.

You frantically run around desperate for more money and frantically buying things to fill that void; however, because there's a hole in your bucket, money keeps running out no matter how much you earn.

One of The Formula's benefits is that you get to See the emptiness you're trying to fill. Then you can Stop yourself from focusing on the mind stories.

The Formula trains you to observe what's going on. It helps you step off the hamster wheel and look at the void you're chasing to fill. No shame. No blame. Just See the void within for what it is without rushing to fill it.

This one simple act is the key to making peace with money.

Stopping and Being Still allows you to surrender to what you're feeling in the moment. It gives you the opportunity you need to go within and check in with your body, to sense where there's contracted energy. From there, you can acknowledge the feeling and release it by breathing into it, so your energy flows more freely.

This gives you space to tap into and experience your internal abundance, and once you experience that, you'll view money in a *whole* new light.

A Whole New Look at Money

Forget what you know about money, for a moment. Ignore the paper and coin form it's become and the number on your bank statement. Detach from expectations of what having it or not having it means.

Stop.

Be Still.

Now consider this—what if money was a relationship. An energetic relationship.

(It is, you know.)

Would you welcome it to your home and give it a reason to stick around, or would you find a reason to push it away?

"Who me? I would never push money away!"
"What if you didn't know you were?"
"How would I know if I was?"

One of my favorite money authors is Ken Honda. Known as the "happy money guy," Ken helps people transform their relationships with money. Here's what he has to say in *Happy Money:*

"Money can absolutely bring us joy.
But, alas, it can also do the opposite. It can bring us stress. And fear. And frustration. And unhappiness. And when it brings those feelings, we may be unconsciously pushing money away.
The more we push it away, the more unhappy we become.[4]"

That was true for me—the more I chased money, the more unhappy I became. And it wasn't until I stopped and observed my patterns and feelings about money and life that I realized I was unconsciously pushing money away.

I didn't have a harmonious relationship with money. I hadn't welcomed it to my home. I always felt the lack of money no matter how much I had. Therefore, money didn't stick around for long.

Now I know that energy is the true currency. What you do with money depends on your emotional connection to money.

Here's more from *Happy Money:*

"Believe it or not, money can be happy. And just not happy, but friendly and smiley.[5]

People's emotional connection to money influences how they earn, spend, and save. It's about the energy you carry, not how much you have or how much you make. It's about how you feel inside.[6]

Learn how to treat money as a welcome guest, allowing it to come and go with respect and without resentment.[7]"

Who do you think money would rather be around—someone with happy energy who welcomes it to their home, or someone with unhappy energy who shuts it out?

Now It's Your Turn

Letting go of money woes begins by examining your relationship with money. Pull out your journal and turn to a blank page or pen your answers here.

Begin by exploring what money means to you. For some, it's what you get from it, such as security, freedom, and status. For others, it's the fun things you can do with it.

Ask yourself, "What does money mean to me?"

_____

_____

_____

_____

_____

_____

Next, take a moment and examine your relationship with money. Is it a good one? Bad one? Ask yourself, "What's my relationship with money?"

_____

_____

_____

_____

_____

_____

Then, ask yourself, "What emptiness am I trying to fill by chasing money?"

_____

_____

_____

_____

_____

_____

Next, "What feelings come up when you think about wanting money?" Some feel anxious. Others feel shame. How about you?

_____

_____

_____

_____

_____

_____

Now, let's shift by looking at all the terrific things money can do for you. Here's what Ken Honda has to say:

> "A husband can surprise his wife with flowers when she's feeling a little blue. A mother can send her children to the college of their choice. A scientist can fund life-saving research. An artist can pursue her dreams of opening her own art studio . . . or an entrepreneur can start the business he's always dreamed of. [9]"

It's your turn. What can money do for you? Better still, ask yourself, "What can I do for others with the money I have?" Now, go on a rampage of gratitude and appreciation and fill a page in your journal.

_____

_____

_____

_____

_____

_____

_____

_____

_____

_____

List three things you'll do to build a happy relationship with money.

1._____

2._____

3._____

How are you feeling?

_____

_____

_____

It's quite natural for strong emotions to emerge at this point. That's fine. Just let them come up. Don't push them down or aside. Instead, pull out your Emergency List and choose which items you need to get relief.

In this situation, which items worked best?

_____

_____

_____

Release and let go.

You make your own luck. ~ Neale Donald Walsch

PART III

From Now On—Everyday Applications of The Formula

Here you'll find suggestions of things you can do right now to Stop yourself from focusing on the mind stories, return to center, and take control of yourself.

CHAPTER 15

Welcome the Monday Blues

Employers are at the happiest on Mondays.
Employees are at the happiest on Fridays.
~ Mokokoma Mokhonoana

Remember "Monday, Monday," the song made famous by the Mamas and the Papas in 1966? How many times have you trailed off singing "Monday, Monday . . ." as you get dressed for the start of your workweek?

Dear reader, if you dread the start of your workweek, you're not alone!

Countless people loathe the idea of getting up on Monday to go to work—especially if your work is an energy-draining nine-to-five job.

No-nonsense motivational speaker, Mel Robbins, knows a thing or two about morning dread.

> "At age 41, my life was a mess. I was unemployed, facing bankruptcy, my marriage was spiraling, and I was hitting the bottle hard. I struggled to get out of bed every morning. The alarm clock would ring. I knew I should get up and deal, but anxiety rushed in, and I'd hit the snooze button instead.[1]"

Can you relate?

I certainly can!

It's called the Monday morning blues. And many people, particularly those with high-stress jobs, experience it after coming off a relaxing, fun-filled weekend.

What Are the Monday Blues?

The start of the workweek, regardless of which day it is, is difficult for many people. While the experience differs, one constant remains the same—there's a clammy dread of foreboding. According to Alexander Kjerulf, one of the world's leading experts on happiness at work:

> The Monday Blues describe a set of negative emotions that many people get at the beginning of the workweek if they're not happy at work. It contains elements of depression, tiredness, hopelessness, and a sense that work is unpleasant but unavoidable. [2]

While most people admit that it takes a bit of time to get into the swing of things on a Monday morning, what's problematic is if the start of your workweek triggers overwhelming feelings of anxiety, sadness, or stress.

My Story

For decades, I dreaded going to work. Not only did I suffer the Monday morning blues, but I also experienced the Tuesday, Wednesday, Thursday, and Friday morning blues! Every. Single. Day. I kid you not, dear reader.

> First thing, as soon as my eyes opened, I'd ask myself two questions: "What day is it?" and "What am I doing today?"

Then, I'd mentally look for something, anything, that would motivate me enough to get up. Lunch with a friend, coffee with convivial colleagues, wearing a new dress or piece of jewelry. Looking forward to the evening when I'd have a Toastmasters meeting or Friday night movies with my family. I looked for anything, no matter how tiny, that would cheer me up a little bit, and nudge me to get out of bed.

Sometimes, dangling a carrot of something I could look forward to was what got me out of bed. Other times, the only thing that did the trick was fearing that I'd be late for work and get fired.

Nonetheless, what ultimately got me out of bed every morning was my boys. I had to get up and go to work for my boys. I had to keep going because of my boys. Otherwise, I'd lose my job and be a bad example for them. My boys were the reason beneath the reason that got me out of bed in the morning.

I chased after anything positive and needed something external to push or entice me out of bed.

Yet, just like taking a pill to dull the pain, what I chased after only lasted for a short time. Then, I'd have to take another one. I was always looking for someone or something out there that would give me a reason to keep going.

It was a terrible way to start my day.

On the weekend or when on holiday, it was much easier to get out of bed. There were more enjoyable things to look forward to; however, no matter how many pleasurable experiences there were, that deep-seated feeling of dread was always with me.

Sometimes the blues came at night. Particularly Sunday night.

Sunday morning, I'd awake happily for another day of spending time with my husband and boys. Then after lunch, things changed. Instead of being present with my family, I'd start thinking about all that needed to be done at work on Monday. Stress crept in as I fretted about upcoming meetings. Waves of anxiety broke against my wall of tranquility as my precious home time ticked away. By the time I went to bed, I was flat-out depressed.

It's hard to believe I actually lived my life this way!

What Causes the Monday Morning Blues?

If you do an internet search on "what causes the Monday blues," you'll find hundreds of ideas; however, the consensus is that it's not just one thing.

You could be suffering from burnout, stuck in a rut, or bored with the routine of things. There's no excitement at work and no room for advancement. You could be resenting having to work, or wishing you could be a stay-at-home mom or dad.

Regardless of the cause, the effects of the Monday blues are far-reaching. At work, you're less productive and more pessimistic. At home, you're less fun and more disengaged from family life. Overall, your creativity suffers, physical activity declines, and social activities wane.

That is, until the weekend. Then you're happy, engaged, and back in touch—it's a rollercoaster of emotional ups and downs.

Help for the Monday Blues

If you do another internet search on "help for the Monday blues'" you'll find an equal number of solutions—everything from getting enough sleep and waking up early, to dressing for success and sticking Post-it Note affirmations on your bathroom mirror.

It doesn't matter whether you change your lifestyle or how many times you tell yourself that your job is just a job, not your life. You can think about positive things all you want, and listen to soothing music on your way to work.

This doesn't last. At least not for long.

Why?

Because you're still chasing something outside of yourself to help you start your day.

My Story

Father of analytical psychology Dr. Carl Jung championed the idea that "What you resist persists." I certainly have found that to be true. The longer or stronger I resist the blues, the longer they persist.

> In 2017 I started meditating every day. And although the intensity of the blues faded a little bit, it wasn't until I started developing the steps of The Formula in 2018 that I finally got a handle on my everyday morning blues.
>
> Now, I no longer resist the blues. Consequently, when they do come along, they often leave gently, without much drama. Now, I See the blues arrive and welcome it. I Stop my mind from trying to make sense of why I'm feeling blue. Instead, I Be Still. I turn inward and feel whatever sensation comes along with the blues. It might be dread, anxiety, sadness,

or even fear. Whatever it is, I allow it to come and feel it. I don't back away. I relax into it. And welcome it like an old friend.

I recognize and acknowledge the blues. I soften my heart and open it, as if there's a door in my heart that I open wide to welcome the blues. Softly, I say, "Hello, blues, you're here again. Thank you. I love you."

Stepping into an appreciation for the blues and the lesson it's teaching me to See, Stop and Be Still, allows me to Shift into a genuine place of gratitude. And when I do that, the blues sensation softens. Although it may linger a little bit, eventually, it goes away.

If it returns on another day, and it will, I work The Formula again. Like a good friend, I let the blues come and go freely. I don't try to keep it away, ignore it, or chase after someone or something else to numb the blues.

What I know is that I can't avoid the Monday blues by looking for and chasing a carrot out there. If I want peace, I have to be at peace with everything that's happening in the present.

Face Your Blues

Does working through the steps of The Formula make the Monday, or any other day, blues permanently go away?

The honest answer is—I don't know. The Formula is a step-by-step process. The more you do it, the more relief you'll have.

What I do know is the best way to stop chasing something is to face it. Straight on. See it for what it is. Stop the mental anguish and go within for peace.

Working through the steps of The Formula and using your Emergency List doesn't guarantee that your life will be all unicorns and rainbows—nothing and no one can make that promise.

What it does is help you See what's here, right now. It trains you to Stop putting your attention on the mind drama and Be Still. It trains you to stop your twirling and focus inward for balance. For only there will you find the peace and strength you seek.

Focus Inward

Remember when you were a child and you'd twirl around and around as fast as you could, making yourself dizzy? Then you'd either stumble after coming out of the twirl or fall while doing it.

Now imagine that you're a professional ballet dancer who does multiple pirouettes for a living. What keeps you from getting dizzy? That's right; you need to focus on one point.

Dear readers, that's what The Formula does—it helps you stop twirling by focusing your attention on an inward point for balance. And once that happens, you can quickly Shift your consciousness to a better feeling place.

Now, when I See that I'm feeling dread, instead of mentally looking for something that will motivate me enough to get up, I Stop and Be Still. Then, I turn inward and feel the sensation that is there.

I Shift by welcoming the dread, opening the door to my heart. All the while, I'm trusting that all is well and that everything is happening for a higher purpose. "Everything is all right. Everything will be all right," is what I tell myself.

Dread will leave as it always does and come back as it will. So be it.

Instead of living in a mental mind field exploding with worry, hopelessness, and dread, The Formula will help you, as it did me, to discover an inner landscape of peace.

Use The Formula to Make Friends

No matter what degree of stress or anxiety you're experiencing, The Formula will help you make friends with the Monday morning blues.

Step One—See the blues for what they are.

Step Two—Stop and Be Still.

> Stop focusing on the mind stories.
>
> Get out of the blues drama by visualizing yourself in the movie theater's balcony *watching* the drama instead of being *in* the drama.
>
> Drop into your body and surrender to the emotion you're feeling.

Step Three—Shift by affirming the situation and say, "thank you."

> As you begin climbing up the vibrational ladder, you'll feel the dread lifting. That's when you know you're making friends with the blues, and welcoming them into your life as you would an old friend.

This is how you'll use The Formula to soften and lessen the Monday morning blues.

See.

Stop and Be Still.

Shift.

Three simple steps.

They're all you need to welcome the Monday blues.

CHAPTER 16

Let Go of the Lies

We are what we think. ~ Buddha

In his *Made in England* album, Elton John sings a song called "Lies." In it, he lists all the things that he and others lie about. We've all been there. We've lied about who we like or dislike. We lied about what we want or don't want.

When we speak our truth, we can feel it coming from a place of knowing. When heard, there's a distinct ring about it. Yet, truth is rarely spoken, and sadly, many truths get swallowed.

It takes courage to speak the truth when you know others will disapprove. It takes conviction to stand up for the truth when those around you disagree.

Still, the truth will set you free, dear reader.

Let's get started!

Lies We *Tell* Ourselves

When it comes to lies, there are two main categories:

1. Lies that we *tell* ourselves.
2. Lies that we *accept* about ourselves.

The first one is easy to spot because we frequently make up stories about ourselves that aren't true. They show up as character-limiting beliefs or "it's not me" lies.

Character lies

We're all familiar with character lies—they're the "I'm not good enough" things we say about ourselves.

Character lies target your self-worth and make a comparison between you and someone else or to a specific standard. These lies erode your character by making you feel bad about yourself.

Every time you put yourself down by saying that you're too fat, too skinny, too tall, or too short, you're making a comparison and telling yourself that you don't measure up to another person or someone else's standard.

Whenever you judge yourself as not pretty enough, not bright enough, too smart, too emotional, or too intense, you're saying that you don't belong, that you don't fit in with a group's standard or norm.

Here's the truth— you are what you think you are.

In the words of Eleanor Roosevelt, "No one can make you feel inferior without your consent." So, stop it!

Limiting belief lies

Limiting belief lies target what you think you can and can't do.

These are lies you tell yourself about yourself.

When you say, "I can't ski, can't play football, don't know how to dance or knit a scarf," these are limiting belief lies. The self-imposed belief that you can't do something. Or could never learn how to do something.

Have you ever found yourself thinking you can't do something even though you've never tried it?

While character lies come about when you compare yourself to another person or standard, limiting belief lies are self-imposed—that you can't do something and that you're not able to change.

"You can't teach an old dog new tricks." Is that true?

When our family immigrated to Canada, my grandmother came with us. To get her citizenship, she had to learn how to speak and write her name in English. The problem with that was my grandmother was illiterate. She never went to school; therefore, she couldn't read or write in Chinese, let alone English. Therefore, we all pitched in to help her become a Canadian citizen.

Talk about teaching an octogenarian dog a new trick!

"It's too late to change careers." Really?

Before becoming a neuro-linguistics programming (NLP) trainer, my teacher, Talis Wong, was a certified engineer working as a civil servant. When he retired, he felt called to teach and became an NLP trainer. For more than a decade, Talis has trained tens of thousands of people in Hong Kong, Macau, and Mainland China.

"I'll never be able to do that." Are you sure?

My cousin Charis thought this, too. For years she'd been wanting to learn how to ride a bicycle while secretly doubting that she ever could. Finally, she plucked up the courage, bought herself a bicycle, and taught herself how to ride it when she was more than fifty years old!

How many times have you told yourself that *if only* you had more money, more time, or more friends to do things with, then your life would be amazing!

Here's the truth you can have, and you can change.

You don't need to be an expert, ready, talented, or experienced before you do something. As Dr. Wayne Dyer reminded us, "The only limitations are the ones you believe."

The "it's not me" lies

Many people blame others and displace responsibility onto other people and situations without even thinking about it. It's automatic.

While character lies are about self-worth, and limited belief lies center on what you can and can't do, "it's not me" lies target accountability.

"It wasn't me!" (When you were in some way responsible.)

"They said to do it." How's that for abdicating responsibility?

"It's not me" lies have at their core a victim mentality. Therefore, when something's wrong, it *can't* be your fault, and the focus quickly shifts to finding someone to blame.

If it's not your fault, you can't be held accountable. Other people and situations are responsible for what happens to you. That's a victim mentality.

There are no consequences because you're not responsible. You can't be blamed because you've done nothing wrong. Therefore, you've nothing to learn from what happened.

Here's the truth—everyone makes mistakes. And it's okay for you to make them. After all, that's the only way for you to learn and grow.

"By seeking and blundering, we learn," declares eighteenth-century writer Johann Wolfgang von Goethe.

Lies We *Accept* About Ourselves

The second category of lies to consider comprises the lies we *accept* about ourselves. This is a little harder to spot because these lies appear to follow a logical sequence of events, even when they don't.

Also called conclusion lies, these are assumptions we jump to when we're around people who are important to us, and we feel insecure.

Let me give you an example:

The situation: Your boss returns work to you asking for some changes.

Conclusion: My *boss* doesn't think I'm good at my job.

In this example, you assumed what your boss thinks concerning your work. Your conclusion seems logical. But is it? Since you didn't fact-check it with your boss, you don't know. Consequently, you accepted a lie about your work that your boss didn't express.

Here's another example:

The situation: Lately, your sweetheart has been withdrawn and distant.

Conclusion: My *sweetheart* is angry with me.

Is that so?

Another:

The situation: Your child cries at night, and you don't go to comfort her.

Conclusion: I'm a lousy parent, letting my *child* cry.

Are you sure about that?

When people important to us are involved, it's easy to jump to conclusions about what they've said, what they've done, and how they're acting.

Maybe you're right. Perhaps you're not. The thing is—you don't know for sure. You've jumped to a negative conclusion about yourself and what you're doing without knowing for sure. It's a conclusion that may or may not be accurate.

Double Whammy

"Okay," I hear you saying, "I have a question: Is it possible to accept lies about ourselves and tell ourselves lies at the same time?"

"Yes!"

That's what I call a double whammy—when the lies we tell ourselves and the lies we accept about ourselves combine for a "one-two punch."

Using a previous example:

The situation: Your boss returns work to you asking for some changes.

Conclusion: My *boss* doesn't think I'm good at my job.

Double whammy: Therefore, I'm not good enough. (Character lie.)

Here's another:

The situation: Lately, your sweetheart has been withdrawn and distant.

Conclusion: My *sweetheart* is angry with me.

Double whammy: It's not my fault. I didn't do anything wrong. ("It's not me" lie.)

Another:

The situation: Your child cries at night, and you don't go to comfort her.

Conclusion: I'm a lousy parent, letting my *child* cry.

Double whammy: I don't know how to be a good parent. (Limited belief lie.)

If you see yourself in any of the above, you're not alone. I'm with you, dear reader!

My Story

When I was in high school, I always walked with my head down. I hung it so low that if you were walking toward me in the hall, all you'd see was the top of my head.

I never raised my head because I was ashamed of the pimples on my face. I thought I was ugly.

My friends tried to help by giving me suggestions about acne medication products and face concealer makeup, which only made things worse. I concluded that *they* were ashamed of how I looked. Whether they were, I don't know. It was a lie I *accepted* about myself.

Therefore, when I went to school and compared myself to all the other girls, I *told* myself that I wasn't pretty enough. That I wasn't perfect. That I didn't deserve to raise my head as I walked down the hall. Talk about a double whammy!

Because of the lies I told and accepted about myself, socially, I had a miserable high school experience. For years, I was ashamed of how I looked, even when I didn't have pimples on my face.

Instead of understanding that it's normal to have pimples as a teenager and chilling out about it, I accepted the lies.

Why We Lie to Ourselves

Often, the lies we tell ourselves are worse than anything anyone could say to us.

I've lost track of the number of times I'd come out of a meeting silently berating myself for saying something wrong, not saying enough, or keeping my mouth shut when I should have said more. My internal monologue was harsh:

> That was stupid.
> What's wrong with you?
> You should have handled that better.

For years I believed the lies I told myself and tried to figure out why. Around I went in my hamster wheel mind asking the same question, over and over again. Until I stepped off the wheel, only then could I see that I had been trying to figure out the wrong thing.

Instead of figuring out *why* I was lying to myself, I needed to Shift my perspective and figure out *what* was true about me.

What. Not why!

What was my truth? Not *why* I was lying about myself.

Eureka!

A New Look at Truth

Believe it or not, it doesn't matter why we lie to ourselves.

I know. A lot of psychologists would say that it does.

(But it doesn't.)

What matters is that we identify the lies we're telling and accepting so we can Shift perspectives and recognize the truth about ourselves. "Change the way you look at things and the things you look at change," according to Dr. Wayne Dyer.

Here's what I know to be true—we're all worthy, limitless beings, capable of taking responsibility for our actions and growing from our mistakes. We're deserving of love and have a great capacity to love. Our true inner state is peace, and happiness is our birthright.

While I don't know how to silence the lies permanently, I do know what will help—The Formula.

Whether you pull out your Emergency List when emotions run hot, and you need to stop your twirling, center, and come back into balance, or you purposefully work through the steps, The Formula changes the narrative of the lies you tell and accept about yourselves.

The Formula moves you away from focusing on your mind stories to surrendering to how your body feels in the moment. Only then can you change how you feel right now.

See.

Stop. Be Still and surrender.

Shift.

Three simple steps.

They're all you need to gain perspective, pause the negative storyline, and change directions.

Today, when I recognize a lie and work through The Formula, I See the lie for what it is. No shame. No blame. I acknowledge its critical nature. Then, I thank it and move on.

Somedays, I poke fun at the lies by telling myself the exact opposite. If I hear myself saying that I'm not good enough, I turn it around and go on a rampage about all the ways I am good enough. Very soon, the heaviness lifts, and the lightness returns.

Years ago, I made a promise to speak the truth about myself. As much as possible. Instead of believing the lies, I would tell myself the truth. And remind me to be kind to myself.

The best way to heal the past, reduce stress, and revitalize yourself is to tell the truth. Your truth.

Now It's Your Turn

In *Radical Honesty,* Dr. Brad Blanton says:

"Freedom is a psychological accomplishment. Only truthfulness will set us free. Many of us already know that in our bones, but we don't always muster the courage to do it.[1]"

Now is the time for you to muster your courage and let go of the lies you tell and accept about yourself.

To begin, pull out your journal and turn to a blank page or pen your answers here. Start by asking yourself, "What are some of the lies I tell and accept about myself?"

_____

_____

_____

_____

_____

_____

Are any of them double whammy lies? If so, write out one of them:
The situation:

_____

Conclusion:

_____

Double whammy:

_____

Identify what kind of lie it is. Is it a lie you *tell* yourself, such as a character, limited belief, or "it's not me" lie? Or is it a lie you *accept* about yourself?

_____

Good. Now that you've identified the lie, it's time to Shift perspective and let your truth soar. Give your truth wings by writing down everything you know to be true about yourself. Write until you can't stop smiling.

_____

_____

_____

_____

_____

_____

_____

_____

_____

_____

_____

List three things that you've learned from telling your truth:

1. _____

2. _____

3. _____

How are you feeling?

_____

_____

_____

It's quite natural for strong emotions to emerge at this point. That's fine. Just let them come up. Don't push them down or aside. Instead, pull out your Emergency List and choose which items you need to get relief.

In this situation, which items worked best?

_____

_____

_____

Release and let go.
And ye shall know the truth, and the truth shall make you free.
~ John[2]

CHAPTER 17

Chase Nothing—Be Happy

Happiness is not a goal; it's a by-product of a life well lived.
~ Eleanor Roosevelt

Chase nothing. Be happy.

If this sounds like a play on Bobby McFerrin's tune, "Don't Worry Be Happy," you're right!

The song's title is from a quote by Indian spiritual master, Meher Baba. McFerrin called it "a pretty neat philosophy in four words," and it inspired him to compose possibly one of the sunniest tunes ever written.

Don't worry.

I agree!

But how, exactly, do you do that?

The key is to chase nothing.

Everyday Battles

Every day, there's an internal battle going on within each of us between what we think will make us happy and what truly will.

As you know from reading this book, when you chase after approval and control of others, when you chase after what happened in the past, façades, outdated success models, and money, what you're actually chasing after is something you *think* will make you happy.

But it doesn't. And it won't. At least not for long.

While you may think that someone or something outside of you will make you happy, deep down inside, you know the truth—think lasting happiness isn't about having something or someone.

"If eating one more piece of chocolate is going to make us happy, then we wouldn't need to eat anymore for the rest of our lives," I once heard Hale Dwoskin, author of *The Sedona Method*, say in an audio program.

Wouldn't that be grand if one more piece of chocolate is all that it took? Or, one more vacation. Another pair of shoes. A better job. A more loving mate.

From reading this book, you know that thinking this way causes you to chase more. And more. Similar to an addict needing one more fix, the wanting doesn't stop. The more won't satisfy. Not for long, anyway.

Here's the caveat—there's nothing wrong with chasing after something *if* the thrill of the chase makes you happy.

What?

I know. I know. It sounds like I'm splitting hairs.

This will help.

Chasing Nothing

I'm a fan of the "Abraham-Hicks" podcasts. I listen a lot and find them uplifting and thought-provoking. One particular story illustrates what I'm talking about:

> "One day Esther was feeling happy and went to the park to eat her lunch. At the park, she sat down on a bench to enjoy her delicious sandwich. She was happy, fully in the moment, and delighting in everything that was happening around her.

Looking around, Esther wondered if everyone else was feeling happy and enjoying the park the same way she was.
Of course, some were. Some weren't.
Esther noticed two types of people in the park: those who were genuinely happy and enjoying their time at the park. And those who weren't. These people were at the park, hoping *the park* would make them feel happy.
While Esther was happy at the park."

Is it clearer now? Do you see the difference?
Chasing nothing versus chasing something.
Esther was chasing nothing. She was present, in the moment, happy with what was. Being at the park was a natural extension of her current state of happiness. She wasn't chasing anything. She was there because she was already happy.
That's what it means to chase nothing. To be in a state, as Abraham-Hicks says, of "Being happy with what is. Eager for more."

Happiness Begins with You

I know this.
You know this.
It's the mind that doesn't.
Instead, the mind tricks you into believing that happiness is out there, somewhere in the future, if only you "do this" or "do that" first.

As soon as I finish cleaning the house, then I'll be able to relax.
If only I could get this project finished, then I'll be able to spend time with my family.

When this pandemic is over, I'll start eating better and exercising.

I'll be happy . . . when.
I'll be happy . . . if.

I'll be happy when I make more money. I'll be happy if I get a raise. I'll be happy if I lose weight. I'll be happy when I buy a new car.

Any future happiness is the mind talking.

Present happiness is wisdom's knowing.

That bears repeating again—any future happiness is the *mind talking*. Present happiness is *wisdom's knowing*.

"Once you know that it is your own mind that is bothering you, and not somebody else, then wisdom dawns," declares Sri Sri Ravi Shankar.

Put Happiness First

Happiness only exists in the moment, never in the future.

You don't need to do something, get something, or experience something to be happy in the present.

Happiness is now.

Happiness comes first.

Be happy in the moment. With what is. Even if what you're experiencing is crappy, find something, *anything* that feels better in the present. Then, work your way up the vibrational ladder to happy. When you do that, happiness stops being a future destination and no longer requires any object or person to make you happy.

It becomes a way of life.

First, See the situation and what you're experiencing for what it is.

Next, Stop yourself from focusing on the mind stories. Then Be Still and surrender to what you're feeling.

Then, pull out your Emergency List and work your way up the vibrational ladder so you can Shift to a place of higher frequency vibration.

Throw in some gratitude and appreciation until you've Shifted to a new vantage point, where new insights and fresh opportunities will present themselves and wisely chosen responses can be made.

Take No Prisoners

What a terrible burden it is when you hold someone else responsible for your happiness.

I'm sure you felt it as a child when your parents expressed their disappointment, and as an adult when you've fallen short of someone else's expectation.

You know how crappy that feels. So, don't place that burden on anyone else. Don't hold anyone hostage. Take no prisoners.

Michael Beckwith reminds us that, "You are at a choice-point in every moment of each circumstance."

"Life is 10% what happens to you and 90% how you react," declares Charles Swindoll.

"How people treat you is their karma; how you react is yours," pronounces Dr. Wayne Dyer.

I like that last one!

Take no prisoners.

Let people be who they are.

Release them from making you happy.

Allow them to be themselves.

As my boys say, "I'll do me, you do you." That's probably the best life advice I've heard—out of the mouths of babes. It's straightforward and clear.

Happiness is up to you. It's for you and certainly something you deserve.

My Story

At the beginning of the year, my helper gave her notice.

If you're not familiar with helpers, they are live-in domestics who assist with housekeeping, cooking, grocery shopping, taking care of the children, and other essential tasks. Helpers are very common in Hong Kong.

> My helper, I'll call her Marta, is very much a part of our family and integral to our household's smooth running. We depend on her.
>
> So, imagine how shocked I was when Marta gave her one month's notice!
>
> At first, I panicked.
>
> How was I going to manage without her? Where was I going to find the time to hire and train someone new? She'd been with our family for six years. My boys adored her. I didn't want to lose her!
>
> My mind tricked me into believing that I needed her to stay.
>
> Consequently, I scrambled by telling her how much she was needed and appreciated. I heaped upon her a mountain of praise. I even tried guilt-tripping her into staying by telling her how much the boys would miss her.

Seriously, dear readers, when my mind freaks out, it's not pretty.

Thankfully, Marta held her ground. She'd made up her mind. She was leaving.

After she left the room, I took a couple of deep, cleansing breaths and pulled out my Emergency List. Little by little, I worked my way up the vibrational ladder. Soon, I felt better. More peaceful. Centered.

In my mind, I flooded Marta with a rampage of gratitude and appreciation for all she had done for our family, not because I was trying to find a way to trick her into staying but because I genuinely felt joyful about all she had done.

"I'll do me. You do you."

Rather than fighting against her decision and chasing after her, I centered myself and let her go.

Be happy with what is.

Take no prisoners.

Relax.

Let God, your higher power, the universe, or however you name it, take it from here.

Be Happy with What Is

Learning how to be happy with what is doesn't mean settling for less or giving up your dreams.

It means getting happy about what you already have and who you love. In other words, stay present. Don't look to the future for something or someone to make you happy, feel loved, secure, or fulfilled. Stay grounded in the present and find things to be happy about that's in your life now.

Rather than longing for something else, appreciate what you have.

Instead of fighting against circumstances, accept them as they are.

"Happiness comes from within. It is not dependent on external things or other people. You become vulnerable and are easily hurt when your feelings of security and happiness depend on the behavior and actions of other people," asserts Dr. Brian Weiss.

Dear reader, what you want is inside you. And it starts with being happy with what is now. Peace, love, joy, happiness, contentment, and belonging, all the things you truly want, are already within you.

Focus on the inside.

Do you!

Only then will "the peace that surpasses all understanding"[1] be yours.

Check In with Happiness

One of my favorite things to do is check in with happiness. Each day, several times during the day, I do a happiness check by asking, "How do I feel?"

From head to toe, I go within and scan myself, looking for both pockets of happiness and areas of tightness within my body where I'm holding stuck energy.

Where I feel contentment and well-being, I smile and inhale through my nose. Where I find pockets of trapped energy, I exhale from my mouth and release.

This exercise helps me stay centered throughout the day and fosters peace and tranquility.

While it only takes a couple of minutes, its benefits are long-lasting and far-reaching.

Ride the Wave

As you know, my family likes going to the beach.

I remember when my boys decided they wanted to learn how to surf. So, my husband and I signed them up for lessons and stood by, watching as they learned how to "pop up" on their boards.

We held our breath and cheered them on as, time after time, they attempted to stand up on the board. It took my boys several days to get the hang of it, with lots of arm flailing and ungainly tumbles as they figured out how to balance on their surfboards.

Like the Weeble that "wobbles, but won't fall down," my boys eventually got centered on their boards and learned how to ride the waves.

That's how it feels when you're happy.

When you check in and realize you're not feeling happy, you can always pop back up on your surfboard, center yourself, and ride the wave.

That's why your Emergency List is so important. It helps you get back on the surfboard after you've tumbled off. Your Emergency List helps you work your way up the vibrational ladder.

That way, you'll never again rely on something or someone outside of you to make you feel happy or good about yourself. You'll be able to do it for yourself.

Now you know why Esther didn't need to chase after the park to make her happy. She was already happy. She was on her surfboard and riding the wave of happiness. Being in the park was part of the wave.

Final Thoughts

Children are remarkably wise.

It's uncanny how they know what to say, exactly when you need it the most.

That's certainly the case with my eldest son.

From an early age, he didn't like it when I was upset. And when I was, he'd demand, "Mommy, be happy!"

Sometimes, that's all it took to Stop me in my tracks so I could Be Still and Shift. Other times, my emotions were too red hot, and I'd lash out with, "You want me to be happy? I'll be happy when you tidy up your room!"

There was a time when I used to think that if my boys behaved as I wanted them to, I'd be happy. Of course, I know better now. And you do, too.

The point of this story is to remind you that The Formula is a process. As Ralph Waldo Emerson reminds us, "Life is a journey, not a destination." While it *will* take you from red-hot emotions to a calm, cool center, it can't jump you there instantaneously.

You have to go through the steps, one by one.

"Start paying attention to how the thoughts feel instead of the content of the thought." That's sage advice from Abraham-Hicks.

> **Step One**—See the situation and what you're experiencing for what it is.
>
> **Step Two**—Stop yourself from focusing on the mind stories. Be Still and surrender to what you're feeling.
> Go inward and check in with your body and sense where there's contracted energy. Then release it by breathing into it, so your energy flows more freely
>
> **Step Three**—Shift by climbing up the vibrational ladder to a place of higher frequency vibration by focusing on what you're grateful for in life. Release and let go.

Above all else, be gentle with yourself.

Your Emergency List is there to put out the flames. The Formula is here to help you "pop up" and center. Because when you're happy, you'll bring joy to the people around you.

Now, go, do you!

When there is light in the soul, there will be beauty in the person.
When there is beauty in the person, there will be harmony in the
house.
When there is harmony in the house, there will be order in the
nation.
When there is order in the nation, there will be peace in the world.
~ Chinese Proverb

Everyday Applications of The Formula Use Ho'oponopono for Reconciliation and Forgiveness

If you're not familiar with Ho'oponopono, it's the ancient Kahuna Hawaiian practice of reconciliation and forgiveness.

Ho'opono means to make right and consists of two words, ho'o (to make) and pono (right). Adding an extra "pono" at the end means to make doubly right, right with yourself and right with others.

I first learned this technique from Marci Shimoff and Debra Poneman when I took their *Year of Miracles* program in 2017. It works so well for me that it's one of my favorite Emergency List techniques.

If you'd like to know more about Ho'oponopono and how you can use it for reconciliation and forgiveness, see the resources section at the end of the book.

Missing the Ferry

It had been a while since my youngest son and I had some one-on-one time together. We both wanted time together, so, the night before, we made plans to take the ferry into Hong Kong. We planned on having lunch at one of his favorite spots.

The following day, I woke up early, eager to get started. My son did not—he was still in bed. You know how teenagers are—they like to sleep!

At noon, I checked on him and he was still asleep!

By this time, I was frustrated, waiting around all morning for him to wake up and irritated that he chose to use our precious "mommy-son" time to sleep in.

Finally, an hour later, he woke up and stumbled into the kitchen, announcing: "I need a shower. We'll take the 2:00 P.M. ferry."

Now I'm fuming.

Ten minutes before the ferry was scheduled to leave, my son emerged from his bedroom, ready to go. Except that we'd have to run to the pier—which I wasn't keen on doing—or we'd miss the ferry.

I exploded!

> Is this how to treat your mother?
> How could you do this to me?
> I waited all morning for you, and now you expect me to *run* to the ferry?
> I don't think so!

Right then, I Saw what was happening. I Stopped, went to my room, and closed my eyes. "Just Stop and Be Still," I told myself, "sense and surrender to the feelings."

As I quieted down, I began letting go of the stories my mind had made up about the situation. I used Ho'oponopono to release the tension and worked my way up the vibrational ladder.

Once I Shifted my perspective, I walked back into the living room and apologized to my son for lashing out at him. We re-grouped and walked to the dock to catch the next ferry. We enjoyed our afternoon together and had a nice lunch.

It took me fifteen minutes to go from red-hot emotions to a calm, cool center, and I'm so glad I did because if I hadn't Seen and Stopped what I was doing, the shouting would have escalated until my son got upset and fired back at me.

Mommy-son time ruined.

Of course, with hindsight, if I'd applied The Formula in the morning when I started stewing about him sleeping in, I would have taken other actions. And never shouted.

LinkedIn Invitation

I received a LinkedIn invitation from someone, I'll call her Mia, that I'd had a run-in with several years ago. Since we'd had a bit of a falling out, I ignored and deleted her first request and was surprised, many months later, when I received a second one.

Why did Mia want to connect with me? Based on what happened in the past, I couldn't imagine why she would.

While I was pondering that question, I realized that I hadn't fully processed the past incident. Although, at the time, I thought I had.

So why was Mia's LinkedIn invitation bothering me?

Over the years, I've learned that when past hurts come back around, it's time to examine them more closely. In Matshona Dhliwayo's book, *The Little Book of Inspiration,* he says this about opportunity:

> "When opportunity knocks a pessimist dials 911.
> When opportunity knocks an optimist sets the table.[1]"

It was time to set the table and open Mia's invitation.

The first thing I noticed was that she had a new job title—it was more prestigious and at a new company.

My mind went crazy making up stories!

> The only reason Mia sent you a second invitation was to brag about her impressive position, to gloat about her latest move to a more prestigious company. She's not interested in connecting with you. She wants to show off: Look at me. Look at me!

Since you've read this far in my book, you know that I grew up believing that I wasn't good enough and that nothing I did was ever enough. That was the primary driver in my life, causing me never to be satisfied and always chase after more.

Memories were being triggered.

With so many decades of accumulated gunk, it's only natural that the opportunity to clear out more of my "not good enough" pockets of stored energy came knocking.

As soon as I Saw that my mind was busy making up drama, I Stopped and Became Still. I went inward, looking for where the stuck pocket of energy was, and sensed that it was somewhere near my solar plexus. It was so intense; it felt as if I had been punched!

I kept my focus there and breathed into the area of trapped energy. As I did, I saw memories flit through my mind. I didn't stop to examine them; I just let them pass by.

As I surrendered to it all, I realized that I was jealous of Mia. She had a new job. She was moving up the career ladder. Without dwelling too much on this realization, I started doing Ho'oponopono to help me get right with myself and get right with Mia. Soon, I was climbing the vibrational ladder and Shifting to a new perspective. Mia was now a guest at my table. I thanked her for coming. And blessed her for giving me the opportunity to reconcile and forgive.

Dear reader, how many times have you inadvertently hurt someone and then felt guilty about it afterward?

If you're like me, more than I care to count.

Ho'oponopono is such an effective technique because not only does it support reconciliation and forgiveness, but it also helps you let go of the afterburn of guilt. The afterburn eats us up inside and continues the cycle of pain on pain.

When you regularly practice Ho'oponopono, you'll put an end to the ouroboros cycle of pain that keeps us feeling worlds apart from the people we love.

How people treat you is their karma; how you react is yours.

~ *Dr. Wayne Dyer*

CHAPTER 19

Everyday Applications of The Formula Use Meditation to Still Your Mind

Meditation has been around for thousands of years. It's a simple technique with long-lasting benefits that will reduce stress and increase calmness, clarity, and well-being. Anyone can meditate. And although there are many different styles, it doesn't matter which one you practice or use. What matters are the results.

As you know from reading *Start Chasing Nothing*, I meditate daily using the Sahaj Samadhi meditation practice from *Art of Living*, and every year I take silent meditation retreats to sit in the silence. The biggest benefit has been the calming of my mind and deep, abiding inner peace.

Outside of my daily practice, I use meditation any time I See that I'm going into hyper-drive with critical thoughts and want to Stop myself from focusing on the mind stories.

Toastmasters

In 2017, I joined Hong Kong's Toastmasters club. Not only did I want to learn how to become a more confident speaker, but I also looked forward to networking and meeting new people.

Each year, the Hong Kong Club has a speech competition where the first-place winner advances to the regional level. That winner then moves to the district level and travels to China, to compete. Although I was new to the club, I liked the idea of going to the mainland to share my message of positivity to a larger audience.

I won at the club level and moved on to the regional competition in 2017.

The night of the competition, I walked up to the podium, centered myself, and gave the best speech of my life.

I was sure I'd won.

Until the next person got up on stage.

From the start, Andy's speech captured the audience's attention. He had great technique and a polished presentation.

Andy won.

Although I did well and came in second, I was utterly deflated. Immediately, my critical mind engaged and started feeding me all kinds of stories:

> What were you thinking? You're not good enough and never were. Andy was better than you. He was more polished. He had all the right gestures. He was funny. You weren't. See, you don't deserve to go to China.

Since I could See what my mind was doing, I quickly Stopped. Became Still. And dropped into my body, feeling for the sadness. All the while, I kept affirming the situation and saying, "thank you."

Thank you for the lesson.

Thank you for the opportunity.

Thank you, God; I know there's a positive side to this.

Tears ran down my face as I made my way home. Still, I affirmed "thank you," trusting that everything was happening for my highest good.

When I arrived home, my family was eager to hear what happened. Choking back tears, I ran past them to my room. There I closed the door, went through the techniques in my Emergency List, and ended with just the thing that helped me most: meditation.

After about ten minutes, I was free of the critical mind and at peace.

I'd climbed up the vibrational ladder and made the Shift from roiling emotions to calm center. All was well. I was at peace and genuinely happy for Andy.

I walked out of my bedroom, calm and centered, and into the dining room where my family and I ate a lovely dinner. I talked about what happened and even laughed about it. Better still, I went to sleep that night, grateful for the experience and happy with the outcome.

The following day, I got a call from the president of my Toastmasters club:

> "Guess what, Elaine? Andy can't go to China. Since you came in second, you automatically advance. You get to go!"

I couldn't believe this was happening!

Just when I had released my attachment to going, the opportunity to go came back around. Without hesitation, I said, "yes!"

Although I didn't win at the district level, I had what I wanted—the opportunity to share my message in front of a larger audience.

While I didn't think my meditating changed the outcome of my going to China, I do know it had a causal effect on my peace of mind. Without that, I would have continued my mental machinations of blaming, complaining, and feeling depressed all evening. I would have missed out on dinner with my family. I would have tortured myself with crazy-making mind stories and robbed myself of a good night's sleep.

Instead, I used meditation to quiet my mind and embrace and accept things as they were in the present moment.

When you wish good for others, good things come back to you.

This is the law of nature. ~ Sri Sri Ravi Shankar

CHAPTER 20

Everyday Applications of The Formula Use Central Channel Breathing to Ground Yourself

I learned how to use Central Channel Breathing to quiet my mind and connect with my body from Dr. Sue Morter. It's a fantastic technique to use when your mind is going crazy and you're finding it difficult to think straight.

Here's how Dr. Morter explains Central Channel Breathing:

> "There is a channel that runs through the center of your body. It has been in existence even before your nervous system developed in the womb. And this channel runs from the top of your head, through the crown center, and right down through the center of the brain, the center of the throat, the center of the chest, down through the center of the belly, down through the pelvis, and drops straight into the earth. With the Central Channel Breath, just imagine that you're moving energy up and down through this channel.
> How?
> Breathing through the nose, imagine the breath starting about two inches above the head, and breathe consciously, right through the center of the brain, through the throat, into the heart, and into the belly.

Breathe in, and make the belly big when you do, and exhale right down through this center, right into the earth. And then a deep breath comes up from the earth into the belly, and exhale, taking your imagination straight up and down through this central channel. This opens the channel and allows us to do so much work.[1]"

Central Channel Breathing is a great way to ground yourself before making important decisions.

My Husband Had an Accident

One beautiful autumn day, I got a call from my husband. I could tell from the tone of his voice that something was wrong. My husband was hurt. At the time of his call, I was in a supermarket in my neighborhood, grocery shopping, many miles away. My husband had been walking in the middle of a footbridge in Central, the business district of Hong Kong, when suddenly, his knee buckled. Immediately, he fell to the ground, unable to get back up.

He needed help.

Immediately, I left the supermarket trolley right where it was, hailed a taxi, and sped to his location. My mind was going crazy with future doom and gloom, flooding me with a tidal wave of panicky "what if" scenarios:

What if something serious has happened? What if he needs surgery? What if he can't walk. What if he can't work? What if I can't get him off the bridge? How will I ever cope?

Right then and there, I Saw my mind racing and knew I needed to Stop focusing on the mind stories. Being Still, I surrender to what I was feeling. Arriving at the footbridge with a freaked-out mind wouldn't help him or me, especially when important decisions would need to be made.

While the taxi driver was navigating his way through traffic, I went to my Emergency List and decided Central Channel Breathing would be just what I needed to quiet my mind.

Breathing in, I drew breath from above my head and channeled it through the center of my brain, my throat, into my heart, and down into my belly. Breathing out, I channeled my breath directly into the earth. With just one cycle, I already felt calmer.

I kept breathing and focusing on the present while moving my breath up and down my channel. Ten minutes later, I felt grounded, centered, and calm. My mind was clear.

When I arrived at the footbridge, my husband was waiting. A kind stranger had helped him up and supported him while he hobbled to the road. Together, we maneuvered him into the taxi and drove to a private hospital.

Two hours later, we were back home. My husband was on crutches with his knee stabilized, and I was still calm and centered.

Do what you can, from what you have, from where you are. ~
Theodore Roosevelt

CHAPTER 21

Everyday Applications of The Formula Let Go of Control for Peace of Mind

Growing up in a family with traditional values, I knew what it meant to be a "good" daughter. Outwardly, I was a model daughter. Inwardly, I was a rebel.

Early in life, I made three vows:

> My father was a lawyer. Therefore, I vowed never to become a lawyer. Besides rebelling against my dad, I think a small part of me didn't think I was smart enough to become a lawyer. So, rather than find out, I vowed never to become one.
>
> My parents had a marriage full of responsibilities and obligations. So, I vowed never to marry and have children. Rather than seeing the beauty in marriage and raising children, I vowed never to have them.
>
> At university, I was on the business administration track. Before choosing a major, we had to take core subjects, such as finance, accounting, and marketing, to see what we liked. Accounting had too much homework. Consequently, I vowed never to become an accountant.

Today, I have a law degree.

I'm married and have two sons.

I'm a certified public accountant.

So much for my vows!

Here's what I've learned: vowing to do something for the wrong reasons won't stop your life from unfolding the way it's meant to be. While the things you do and experiences you have may appear to be random, you'll see how the dots are connected when you look back.

White Water Rafting in Scotland

One summer, our family went to Scotland on holiday. My husband grew up in Scotland, he knows the area well, and wanted us to go white water rafting.

My boys and I were up for that, so off we went.

As we took our places in the raft, our rafting guide went through the safety check, telling us what to do if we fell out of the boat:

Flip over on your back.

Act like a turtle.

Tuck in your arms.

Relax, and go with the flow.

"Don't struggle against the current or try to grab onto anything," he warned, "Let the river take you. Eventually, you'll end up in calm waters."

Dear reader, isn't that a great analogy for life?

Don't struggle. Be happy.

In the river of life, everything works out when you go with the flow—recognizing that when the unexpected happens, in the end, calm waters are there waiting for us.

Here's what I've learned—accepting people and events as they are is the way the river of life works best. Swimming against the current will beat you up, wear you down, and sap your energy. Go with the flow, and you'll arrive at your destination refreshed and ready to go.

Sometimes letting things go is an act of far greater power
than defending or hanging on. ~ Eckhart Tolle

CHAPTER 22
Everyday Applications of The Formula From One Parent to Another

At birth, something equally magical and disquieting occurs. The moment our babies snuggle into our arms, we feel the full weight of parental responsibility while marveling at the new life we've created.

Becoming a parent is not a singular event.

It's a generational one.

When we become parents, we carry within our own beliefs about parenting, the generational imprinting of how we were parented. And we deposit upon our newborns all the hopes, well wishes, good intentions, and expectations of generations of parents who have gone before us.

We also heap upon them layers of expectations, guilt, and regret. We want to do a better parenting job than our parents did—even if they did a great job!

Because of this, we become hyper-concerned, overly critical, and heavily invested in our children's lives—especially if you're a tiger mom, like me!

Vicious Cycle
Parents hold themselves to impossible standards. And even higher ones for their children.

As parents, we have expectations of our children based on our own beliefs of what "good" parenting means. These expectations inform our children how to behave and act, not only to be productive citizens of the world, but also because doing so reflects on us as parents.

Having a well-behaved child means I'm a good parent. Right? Conversely, when my child acts out, it means I've done something wrong. We blame our children when they don't do what we want them to do, then feel guilty for not doing a good enough job as parents. We take responsibility for their shortcomings and regret that we didn't do enough or spend enough quality time with them. This sets them and us up for a vicious cycle of action and reaction. Each action adds a layer of pain. Each reaction adds another layer of pain. Like an ouroboros eating its tail, it is an endless cycle.

We blame. Our children cry.

We feel guilty. Our children distance themselves from us.

We regret and double down by lashing out. Our children rebel.

It's a rancorous cycle, hurtful to our children and us.

While it's challenging to separate our children from ourselves, it's something we must do as parents.

Our children are their own people. They instinctively know what's right for them and what they need to grow into the adults they're to become. As Dr. Seuss says, "A person is a person, no matter how small."

Children Growing Up

As my boys got older, they naturally pushed back against the over-governance and structure that I provided. They wanted to make their own decisions and, if there were consequences, learn from them. Sounds healthy, right?

But how do you do that without feeling guilty?

One day, my neuro-linguistic programming (NLP) teacher, Talis Wong, offered this analogy:

> "You go to the market in search of oranges. You look for the very best ones, turning them over and smelling each for freshness and sweetness. Finally, you find six oranges that meet your standard. You put them in your bag, pay for them, and go home.
>
> All the while, you're thinking of these beautiful oranges and how much your family will enjoy eating them.
>
> Once home, as you're taking them out of the bag, you notice that one of the oranges has a soft spot. And when you gently press, it's mushy. "Oh-oh," you groan, "Looks like one of the oranges is going off."
>
> What went wrong?
>
> Nothing!
>
> When you went to the market, you picked out the finest oranges you could find. Under the circumstances, you did your best. So, why blame yourself for doing your best?"

Sadly, many parents blame themselves when they think their best isn't good enough. They're overly self-critical, lash out when their children don't do as expected, then feel guilty afterward.

Fellow parents, it's this cycle that we must break.

Here's what I want you to know—you're doing your best. Be gentle with yourself when things don't turn out as planned. Let go of the guilt and blame. Use your Emergency List to Shift perspective and move on without adding to the pain cycle.

Only then can the generational pain that we've inherited stop. Only then can both you and your children be freed.

You're just a few laughs away from letting a whole lot of good stuff in. You're just a few kisses away from letting a whole lot of good stuff in. You're just a little bit of relief away from letting a whole lot of good stuff in. ~ Abraham-Hicks

CHAPTER 23

Everyday Applications of The Formula Daily Things to Do

Throughout the day, there are things you can do that will help you stay centered and present. One thing they all have in common is that they're simple, quick, and beneficial. You can use them when you feel a small mind story brewing, or when you're full-out panicking.

I've used these nine things for several years and can attest to their effectiveness—you'll notice that several of them are on my current Emergency List.

Try them out for yourself. Use them singularly or in combination. Use them when you need a little boost throughout the day, or as an entrée into The Formula. There's no right or wrong here. Whatever works for you is best for you.

In no particular order, here's my "go-to" list of nine daily things I do that will help you, too.

Keep an Eye on the Inside

During the day, whenever it crosses my mind, I turn inward and check how I'm feeling on the inside. I quickly scan for areas of contraction and immediately clear them. I do this by slowly breathing as I focus on the contraction while relaxing my body.

Soften Your Heart

I learned how to soften my heart from my coach, Suzanne Lawlor. You can also find this technique in Michael A. Singer's book, *The Surrender Experiment.*

> "Hover your hand over your heart. Feel the space outside your heart area.
>
> Now, close your eyes and focus your attention inward, from outside your heart area to inside your heart area. Slowly, lower your hand.
>
> From that space, move energy upward to your head, passing through your throat. Then, move energy into your chest and belly. Notice that there's no boundary between the inside and outside of your heart space. Also, that it's quiet and peaceful inside and out.
>
> Return your attention to your inner heart space. Open your eyes and notice that the inner heart space is still there. It's peaceful. Quiet. Soft.[1]"

Whenever you are experiencing emotional turmoil, tune into your inner heart space for peace. From there, you can scan for contracted energy and breathe into these areas until you feel more expanded and aligned.

You can get the same benefit if you're in public; just keep your eyes open.

Your inner heart space is home. For me, it's the green pasture that's talked about in Psalm 23.

Use One Second at a Time to Restore Sanity

It's so effective that it's often the first thing I do on my Emergency List because it stops my twirling and focuses my attention inward for balance.

It's also a fantastic technique when you're in an intense situation or dealing with severe emotional pain. When your mind is hyper-reacting, churning out crazy-making scenarios, and the enormity of it all is overwhelming you.

But you can handle one second.

Remember this, dear reader—you *can* handle one second.

As soon as you See yourself focusing on mind stories, Stop. Be Still and go inward. Focus attention either on your heart or on your breathing.

Then, repeat to yourself, "Just focus on this one second. One second at a time."

Soon, sanity returns, and you'll feel calmer.

How Does It Get Any Better Than This?

My mentor, Debra Poneman, taught me the value of asking: "How does it get any better than this?"

Debra first learned about this pivotal question from Dain Heer while taking an Access Consciousness course.[2] As a result, she recommends asking this question not only when things are going well, but especially when they're not.

The nifty thing about asking this question is that it takes you out of your left brain, the logical thinking hemisphere, and positions you in the right hemisphere side of the brain—the place where curiosity resides.

When you tap into curiosity, your brain floods your body with dopamine—making you feel happier!

This is such a clever way for you to gain control so you can Shift and move up the vibrational ladder.

Read Uplifting Quotations

Distract yourself by reading uplifting quotations or sayings. Anything you have on hand will do. And you'll immediately do a mental Shift.

For example, when I feel upset by what other people say or do, I remind myself of one of my favorite quotations from Dr. Wayne Dyer: "How others treat me is their karma; how I react is mine."

When You Need to Let Go of Feelings

This is my favorite go-to technique when I need to release and let go. Developed by Dr. David R. Hawkins, it comes from his book *Letting Go:*

> "Letting go involves being aware of a feeling, letting it come up, staying with it, and letting it run its course without wanting to make it different or do anything about it.
>
> It means simply to let the feeling be there and to focus on letting out the energy behind it.
>
> The first step is to allow yourself to have the feeling without resisting it, venting it, fearing it, condemning it, or moralizing about it. It means to drop judgment and see that it is just a feeling.
>
> The technique is to be with the feeling and surrender all efforts to modify it in any way.

Let go of wanting to resist the feeling. It is resistance that keeps the feeling going.

When you give up resisting or trying to modify the feeling, it will shift to the next feeling and be accompanied by a lighter sensation. A feeling that is not resisted will disappear as the energy behind it dissipates.[2]"

When You're Feeling Angry or Critical

Tell yourself: "When I condemn, I hurt me. When I let go, I set me free."[3]

When You Need Help

One year when we were on a ski holiday, I slipped on the ice and twisted my ankle. Immediately, my husband and the boys hoisted me up and helped me walk back to the hotel. Since then, whenever we come across an icy path, we would huddle up, and walk arm in arm, shouting (and laughing,) "Eight legs are better than two!" Such a sweet reminder that we all need help from time to time. So, call out to God, your higher power, or the universe for assistance. Reach out to your angels, or spirit guides, or ancestors for help, and trust they'll be there when you do.

Go on now. Grab a friend. Make a call. Give yourself permission to ask for help.

Giddy with Gratitude.

Whenever you think about it, make a list of things that you're grateful and thankful for every day. It's from Debra Ponemen that I learned about the power of gratitude.

When good things happen, say thanks. When bad things happen, still say thanks. Thanks to God, the universe, your higher power, or however you name it. Thanks for the teaching and whatever lessons you're supposed to learn.

Go on a rampage of thanks till you're feeling giddy with gratitude.

The more you appreciate and celebrate your life,
the more there is in life to celebrate. ~ Oprah Winfrey

Overview of The Formula

See.

Stop and Be Still.

Shift.

As soon as you feel negative emotion, See what you're experiencing. Stop yourself from focusing on the mind stories. Be Still and surrender to what you're feeling.

Notice where you feel the contraction in your body. Do you feel tightness in your chest, pressure on your forehead, or a sickness in your stomach?

Focus your attention in that area and surrender to that sensation by taking long deep breaths and directing your breath. This focused attention, coupled with intentional breathing, is what helps you let go of resisting what is happening in the moment. After you feel calmer, start climbing the vibrational ladder.

Three simple steps that will profoundly impact your life.

Step One—See

To See means to become aware of the emotional fire within you. You can't put out the flames until you See and identify what the fire is, and where it's living within your body.

Step Two— Stop and Be Still

To Stop and Be Still means stopping yourself from focusing on the mind stories. Then Be Still and surrender to what you're feeling.

Remember; your mind recalls the past and projects into the future, while your body resides in the present moment. Therefore, Stop and Be Still to prevent your mind from engaging with past stories or future worries. It's about interrupting your attention on the mind stories so that you can Stop and Be Still in the present moment.

Once you've done that, check in with your body and sense where there's contracted energy. Follow the sensation and identify where it is in your body. Recognize how you're feeling, acknowledge the feeling, then release it by breathing into it, so your energy flows more freely.

While you're doing this, make no judgments. Instead, say, "I'm okay. Everything's okay. I trust that all is well."

Step Three—Shift

To Shift means to begin climbing up the vibrational ladder to a place of higher frequency vibration, to a place of joy and positivity where you're focused and happy.

The Shift to climb up the vibration ladder differs depending on the person as well as the situation. That's why having an Emergency List is so helpful!

One of the first things you'll notice is that you're reacting less to what initially upset you, and you're feeling more kind-hearted to others and gentle with yourself.

Soon, you'll feel within your body the sensations of expansion and openness. You'll release and go with the flow, rather than resisting and pushing against things.

Sometimes, the Shift is made possible through gratitude. Other times, through love.

Shifting through gratitude is very powerful because when you focus on what you're grateful for in life, your attention organically Shifts from what upsets you to what makes you feel happy.

Shifting through love is tremendously healing because it can include forgiveness—of others and for yourself. If you're in a situation where you're distressed by what someone has done, it may be forgiveness that will take you up the ladder so you can Shift to a higher vibration.

Now that you've Shifted to a new vantage point, new insights and fresh opportunities will present themselves, and wisely chosen responses can be made.

All is well.

You're light and free.

Go in peace and love.

Be happy.

Start. Chasing. Nothing.

Elaine Chung, August, 8, 2021

NOTES

Preface

[1] Lisa Feldman Barrell, Ph.D., *How Emotions Are Made: The Secret Life of the Brain* (New York: Houghton, Mifflin, Harcourt, 2017), Kindle.

[2] Ibid.

[3] Stephen R. Covey, *7 Habits of Highly Effective People* (New York: Simon & Schuster, 1989), 299.

[4] The Merriam-Webster Dictionary (2016), s.v. "Aha Moment."

[5] Stephanie Vincenty, "Oprah Explains What an 'Aha Moment' Really Means," *Oprah Daily*, September 19, 2019, https://www.oprahdaily.com/life/a29090436/aha-moment-meaning/.

Introduction

[1] Stephen King, *On Writing* (New York: Simon & Schuster, 2000), 249.

Chapter 2

[1] Joseph Campbell, Ph.D., *The Hero with a Thousand Faces* (New Jersey: Princeton University Press, 1973), Kindle.

Chapter 3

[1] J l ad-D n Mohammad R m, *Rumi Poetry: 100 Bedtime Verses* (Createspace Independent Publishing Platform, 2017), Kindle.

[2] Phil. 4: 7 NIV (New English Version).

Chapter 4

[1] Nori St. Paul, "Naples Woman Devoted to Helping Save, Adopt Out Retired Greyhound Racers." *Naples Daily News,* July 18, 2015, http://archive.naplesnews.com/lifestyle/neapolitan/naples-woman-devoted-to-helping-save-adopt-out-retired-greyhound-racers-ep-1191319325-337527951.html.

Chapter 5

[1] Marci Shimoff, *Happy for No Reason: 7 Steps to Being Happy from the Inside Out* (New York: Atria Books, 2009), 132.

Chapter 6

[1] Tom Cronin, "The Stillness Project," accessed April 6, 2021, https://stillnessproject.com/about.

Chapter 7

[1] Ram Dass, "Being Love" *Ram Dass Foundation,* accessed April 7, 2021. https://www.ramdass.org/being-love.

[2] 1 Cor. 13: 4-7 NIV (New English Version).

[3] Ibid., 13.

[4] Yael Eylat-Tanaka, *The Book of Values: An Inspirational Guide to Our Moral Dilemmas* (Yael Eylat-Tanaka, 2014), chap. Gratitude, Kindle.

[5] "Giving Thanks Can Make You Happier," *Harvard Health Publishing,* accessed July 13, 2021, https://www.health.harvard.edu/healthbeat/giving-thanks-can-make-you-happier.

[6] Anne Lamott, *Plan B: Further Thoughts on Faith* (New York: Riverhead Books, 2006), 47.

[7] Anne Lamott, *Traveling Mercies: Some Thoughts on Faith* (New York: Anchor Books, 1999), 134.

Chapter 8

[1] Reinhold Niebuhr, "Prayer for Serenity," Celebrate Recovery, accessed April 7, 2021, https://www.celebraterecovery.com/resources/cr-tools/serenityprayer.

[2] Ps. 23: 1-6 ESV (English Standard Version).

Chapter 9

[1] Gareth Cook, "Why We Are Wired to Connect," *Scientific American*, October 22, 2013, https://www.scientificamerican.com/article/why-we-are-wired-to-connect/.

[2] The Merriam-Webster Dictionary (2016), s.v. "Self-Worth."

Chapter 10

[1] Aesop, *The Aesop for Children with Original Pictures by Milo Winter* (New York: Rand McNally & Co, 1919), Library of Congress.

[2] Ken Poirot, *Mentor Me: GA=T+E—A Formula to Fulfill Your Greatest Achievement* (Indianapolis: Dog Ear Publishing, 2014), Kindle.

[3] Deepak Chopra, M.D., *The Seven Spiritual Laws of Success: A Practical Guide to the Fulfillment of Your Dreams* (San Rafael, CA: Amber-Allen Publishing, 1994), Kindle.

[4] Matt. 7:3 ESV (English Standard Version).

[5] The Merriam-Webster Dictionary (2016), s.v. "Accepting."

Chapter 11

[1] Eyal Winter, Ph.D., "Why It Is Hard to Live for the Moment," *Psychology Today*, September 19, 2016, https://www.psychology-today.com/us/blog/feeling-smart/201609/why-is-it-hard-live-the-moment.

Chapter 12

[1] Katty Kay & Claire Shipman, *The Confidence Code: The Science and Art of Self-Assurance — What Women Should Know* (New York: Harper-Collins Publishing, 2014), 164.

[2] The Merriam-Webster Dictionary (2016), s.v. "Authenticity."

[3] Don Miguel Ruiz, *The Four Agreements: A Practical Guide to Personal Freedom* (San Rafael, CA: Amber-Allen Publishing, 1997), 8.

[4] Brené Brown, Ph.D., "The Power of Vulnerability," filmed June 2010 in Houston, U.S.A., TED video, 20:03. https://www.ted.com/talks/brene_brown_the_power_of_vulnerability?language=en.

Chapter 13

[1] Debra Poneman, *The 5 Secrets to a Life of True Success* (Debra Poneman, 2020), 4, PDF.

[2] The Merriam-Webster Dictionary (2016), s.v. "Success."

[3] Jacquelyn Smith, "This Is How Americans Define Success," *Business Insider*, October 3, 2014, https://www.businessinsider.com/how-americans-now-define-success-2014-10.

[4] Arianna Huffington, *Thrive: The Third Metric to Redefining Success and Creating a Life of Well-Being, Wisdom, and Wonder* (New York: Harmony, 2014), Kindle.

[5] Ibid.

[6] Madison Lennon, "10 Things George Clooney Does to Achieve Success," *The Richest,* October 16, 2019. https://www.therichest.com/luxury/george-clooney-success-tips/.

[7] Max Ehrmann, *The Desiderata of Happiness* (New York: Crown Publishers,1948), 10.

Chapter 14

[1] Kyle Cease, *The Illusion of Money: Why Chasing Money Is Stopping You from Receiving It* (Carlsbad, CA: Hay House, 2019), Kindle. https://kylecease.com/illusion/

[2] Ibid.

[3] Heb. 13:5 ESV (English Standard Version).

[4] Ken Honda, "Happy Money: The Japanese Art of Making Peace with Your Money," accessed April 5, 2021, https://kenhonda.com.

[5] Ibid.

[6] Jill Cornfield, "Zen millionaire Ken Honda Says Your Personality Type Is Key to How You Handle Your Finances," *CNBC*, August 9, 2019, https://www.cnbc.com/2019/08/09/do-you-recognize-yourself-in-one-of-these-emotional-money-types.html.

[7] Honda, "Happy Money," https://kenhonda.com/book.

[8] Ibid," https://kenhonda.com.

Chapter 15

[1] Mel Robbins, "About Mel," accessed July 12, 2021, https://melrobbins.com/about/.

[2] Jacquelyn Smith, "11 Ways to Beat the Monday Blues," *Forbes*, February 25, 2013, https://www.forbes.com/sites/jacquelynsmith/2013/02/25/11-ways-to-beat-the-monday-blues/?sh=56b2d5f023f5.

Chapter 16

[1] Brad Blanton, Ph.D., *Radical Honesty: How to Transform Your Life by Telling the Truth* (Stanley, VA: Sparrowhawk Publications, 1994), 282.

[2] John 8:32 KJV (King James Version).

Chapter 17

[1] Phil. 4:7 NIV (New English Version).

Chapter 18

[1] Matshona Dhliwayo, *The Little Book of Inspiration* (Toronto: Wise Words from a Foolish Son., 2016), Kindle.

Chapter 20

[1] Sue Morter, D.C., "Central Channel Breathing," last modified August 1, 2014, https://drsuemorter.com/2014/08/01/the-central-channel-breath/.

Chapter 23

[1] Michael A. Singer, *The Surrender Experiment: My Journey into Life's Perfection* (New York: Harmony, 2015), Kindle.

[2] David R. Hawkins, M.D., Ph.D., *Letting Go: The Pathway of Surrender* (Carlsbad, CA: Hay House, 2014), 32.

[3] "About," Access Consciousness, accessed June 25, 2021, https://www.accessconsciousness.com/en/about/.

RESOURCES

This section includes a list of books, programs, techniques, and websites that I've used and found helpful.

The books may be found at your local bookstore, favorite online retailer, or directly from the author's website. In some cases, they can be downloaded to your e-reader or listened to through your preferred listening device.

All programs and techniques have direct URL links, current as of this publication date.

Books

Rajita Kulkarni Bagga, *The Unknown Edge: A Mystical Journey of Self-Discovery*

Dale Carnegie, *How to Stop Worrying and Start Living*

Jack Canfield, The *Success Principles*

Deepak Chopra, *The Seven Spiritual Laws of Success*

Alan Cohen, *A Course In Miracles Made Easy*

Stephen R. Covey, *The 7 Habits of Highly Effective People*

Dr. Joe Dispenze, *Breaking the Habit of Being Yourself: How to Lose Your Mind and Create a New One*

Dr. Wayne Dyer, *Change Your Thoughts — Change Your Life: Living the Wisdom of the Tao*

Dr. Wayne Dyer, *The Power of Intention: Learning to Co-Create Your World Your Way*

Neville Goddard, *The Power of Awareness*

Neville Goddard, *Be What You Wish*

Dr. David R. Hawkins, *Power vs. Force: The Hidden Detriments of Human Behavior*

Dr. David R. Hawkins, *Letting Go: The Pathway to Surrender*

Louise Hay, *You Can Heal Your Life*

Steven Hagen, *Buddhism Plain and Simple: The Practice of Being Aware Right Now, Every Day*

Napoleon Hill, *Think and Grow Rich*

Byron Katie, *Loving What Is*

Sarah McCrum, *Love Money, Money Loves You: A Conversation with the Energy of Money*

Dr. Sue Morter, *Energy Codes: The 7-Step System to Awaken Your Spirit, Heal Your Body, and Live Your Best Life*

Dr. Joseph Murphy, *The Power of Your Subconscious Mind*

Dr. Joseph Murphy, *Powers of Meditation*

Dr. Susan L. Reid, *Discovering Your Inner Samurai: The Entrepreneurial Women's Journey to Business Success*

Derek Rydall, *Emergence: Seven Steps for Radical Life Change*

Florence Scovel Shin, *The Game of Life and How to Play It*

Florence Scovel Shin, *Your Word is Your Wand*

Marci Shimoff, *Happy For No Reason*

Sri Sri Ravi Shankar, *An Intimate Note to the Sincere Seeker*

Michael A. Singer, *Untethered Soul: The Journey Beyond Yourself*

Michael A. Singer, *The Surrender Experiment: My Journey into Life's Perfection*

Eckhart Tolle, *A New Earth: Awakening to Your Life's Purpose*

Eckhart Tolle, *The Power of Now: A Guide to Spiritual Enlightenment*

Wallace D. Wattles, *The Science of Getting Rich*

Paramahansa Yogananda, *Autobiography of a Yogi*

Programs

A Course in Miracles

This unique spiritual self-study program is designed to awaken you to the truth of your oneness with God and love.

https://acim.org/

The Art of Living Foundation

The Art of Living Foundation offers a complete meditation experience, breathwork, inspiration, and guidance to live a happy life.

https://www.artofliving.org/us-en

I particularly recommend their Happiness Program, which teaches Sudarshan Kriya (SKY) breath meditation.

https://www.artofliving.org/happiness-program

CMA International Foundation

CMA International Foundation is a unitary, non-denominational, faith-based community church open to all seekers.

https://masterangels.org/about/

Health Beyond Belief

Begun by John Newton, Health Beyond Belief is for anyone seeking a life free from physical and emotional pain. Also, ancestral clearing.

https://healthbeyondbelief.com/

Self-Realization Fellowship

Founded by Paramahansa Yogananda, the Self-Realization Fellowship is where "you'll realize that all along there was something tremendous within you, and you didn't know it."

https://yogananda.org/

The Work of Byron Katie

The Work provides a pathway to meet your internal wisdom.

https://thework.com

Your Year of Miracles

Founded by my mentors Marci Shimoff and Debra Poneman, and now also includes Dr. Sue Morter and Lisa Garr, you'll learn how to live your life in the Miracle Zone.

https://youryearofmiracles.com/mp/miracles-in-2021/

Yes to Success

Begun by my mentor, Debra Poneman, Yes to Success shows you how to live a profoundly joyful and truly successful life.

https://yestosuccess.com

Techniques

Abraham-Hicks

https://www.abraham-hicks.com/

The Art of Living's Sahaj Samadhi meditation

https://www.artofliving.org/us-en/sahaj-samadhi-meditation

Ho'oponopono

https://www.laughteronlineuniversity.com/hooponopono-4-simple-steps/

Dr. Sue Morter's Central Channel Breathing

https://m.youtube.com/watch?v=3JKz4V9V4Xk

The Sedona Method

https://www.sedona.com/Home.asp

ABOUT ELAINE CHUNG

Elaine Chung's passion for happiness and an uplifting message of growth gives hope and positivity to the world.

Elaine is co-author of *You Lead You* and presents corporate training workshops on leadership development. She helps people lead themselves with inner conviction and outward confidence.

Elaine is an award-winning speaker. Her uplifting message advocates the power of having a positive mindset and turning inward for peace and happiness.

In addition to being a certified public accountant, Elaine holds an executive diploma in corporate coaching and is working on becoming an NLP Master Practitioner.

Elaine describes herself as an ordinary woman living an ordinary life who's found a simple way to return to happiness and peace. She lives in Hong Kong with her husband and family.

If you'd like to contact Elaine, please do so at: Elaine@startchasing-nothing.com.

Repose in silence
Surrender to receive all
Start chasing nothing
—Elaine Chung

ABOUT DR. SUSAN L. REID

Susan Reid takes the fear out of writing so that you can get your book published and read by adoring fans. And touch those who need it.

Susan left academia in 2004 after a successful career as a professor and conductor to found Alkamae. Alkamae exists to help creative women grow their small businesses through the written word.

Specializing in book manuscripts, articles for publication, and web copy, Susan focuses on writing creative nonfiction for aspiring authors—true stories, well told.

She helps authors turn their dreams into reality and passion into publication with her creative writing acumen.

To connect with Susan and inquire about her writing, please contact Susan at Alkamae.com.

Success is assured,
Greatness is,
Beauty surrounds, and
All is well.